FOREVER AFTER
An Ever After Romance

Linda Poitevin

Michem Publishing, Canada

Published by Michem Publishing, Canada

This is a work of fiction. Names, characters, places, and incidents are the sole product of the author's imagination or are used fictitiously. Any resemblance to actual persons, living or dead, business establishments, events, or locations is coincidental.

FOREVER AFTER
Copyright 2015 by Linda Poitevin

Cover art by Kanaxa
Interior Design by Clara Stone

All rights reserved.

No part of this book may be reproduced, scanned, or distributed in any printed or electronic form without written permission.

Purchase only authorized editions. Thank you for respecting the author's work and not supporting or encouraging piracy. To obtain permission to excerpt portions of the text, please contact the author at info@lindapoitevin.com

ISBN: 978-1-9894570-2-3

Chapter 1

"You know you're just being stubborn about not hiring a housekeeper, right?"

Gwynneth Jacobs' heart kicked against her ribs as she looked over her shoulder at the man framed in the bathroom doorway. Broad-chested, dark-haired, and with the banked heat in his deep brown gaze that still made her world tilt on its axis, even after months of living together. Especially after he'd been away for the last three weeks.

"You're home," she said, choosing to state the obvious rather than respond to—and rehash yet again—the same argument they'd been having since he moved in. "And you're early. I wanted to have the house clean before you got here." She cast a rueful glance at her shirt, wet from her tub-cleaning efforts. "I was hoping to have me clean, too."

Gareth Connor's mouth tipped up at the corner, telling her he knew perfectly well she avoided his question. "I caught an earlier flight, but I can leave and come back again, if you'd rather. Or..."

Gwyn's heart did another flip. A familiar, slow

warmth kindled in her belly. She took the hand Gareth stretched out to her and let him pull her to her feet. "Or?"

He tugged her close, hands spanning her waist, until her hips rested against his. "Or I could just help you get clean. You know, wash your back and all those hard to reach places..."

One hand traced her spine from top to bottom, and Gwyn inhaled on a sharp hiss. She leaned into him, hungry for the touches missing from her life for the better part of a month. Being almost married to a Hollywood mega star who did this much traveling was harder than she'd thought it would be.

Gareth buried his face in her hair. "God, I missed you, Gwynneth with two n's," he growled against her neck.

"I missed you, too," she whispered. While this latest absence had been far from his first since moving in with her and the kids, having him away hadn't become any easier. Every single day without him seemed an eternity that no number of phone calls and late night conversations could ease.

Gareth's lips parted hers, sending the world spinning away in a whirl of need, a rush of desire. Forgetting all about the damp of her shirt and the rubber gloves she still wore, Gwyn wrapped her arms around his neck and held on to the only anchor she had. The only thing that mattered in that moment. Somewhere in the distance, a door slammed.

"Mommy! We're home!" Katie's voice called out from the bottom of the stairs.

UNEXPECTED COMPLICATIONS

A shout stopped her. "Hey! You can't go back there! Stop!"

The bridal shop attendant frowned and reached for the door knob. For a split second, Gwyn froze. Then, in the space of a heartbeat, she knew. She spun around, clutching the dress to herself with one hand and reaching out with the other.

"No! Don't—"

Too late. The attendant had already turned the handle. The door burst open, knocking her into the wall, and a camera flash blinded Gwyn. Once. Twice. Three times. Gwyn threw up a hand to shield her eyes.

"Smile for me, Gwyn, there's a girl!" a cheerful male voice said. "Let's have a look at that pretty dress of yours."

"Get out get out get out!" Carol's voice shrieked, accompanied by what sounded like repeated smacks.

"Ow! Easy does it, love," the man complained. "I have what I need. I'm leaving, already!"

Gwyn blinked past the spots in her vision to see the photographer ducking away from Carol's attack, back-peddling out of the fitting room. The event assistant chased him out into the store, and Gwyn stood, stunned and disbelieving, unable to move if she'd tried. Unable to think.

Gareth's mouth stilled. His arms tightened. Gwyn braced herself for the loss of his warmth. He pulled back and looked down at her ruefully. "I see nothing has changed in my absence. They were out with Kristin?"

"She took them to the park so I could get the cleaning done."

"And she couldn't have kept them there another fifteen minutes?" He half groaned, half sighed as he disentangled himself. "We need to work out some kind of signal with that girl."

"What, like a necktie on the door knob?" Gwyn grinned and planted a kiss on his chin. "Aren't we a little old for that?"

"Mommy?" Katie called again.

"We will never be too old for that." Gareth reached out to trace a thumb over her lips, sending a fresh ripple through her. "Rain check?"

"Rain check," Gwyn agreed. She cleared the huskiness from her throat, then responded to her daughter. "Upstairs, Katie. I'm cleaning the bathroom. And guess who's home?"

"Gareth!" three voices squealed in unison. Feet thundered up the stairs toward them.

Gareth chuckled. "Duty calls. I'll let you finish up here while I hand out presents, shall I?"

"I thought we agreed you wouldn't bring back gifts every time you went away."

"*You* agreed. *I* told you that you were a spoilsport." Gareth staggered under the assault of three little bodies. "Whoa! Easy does it or you'll knock me over, and I won't be able to open my suitcase, and then what?"

"You brought us presents?" Nicholas released his hold on Gareth's legs to dance a little jig. "Yes!"

"I lost a tooth!" Maggie tipped back her head and opened her mouth wide for Gareth's inspection. "And the tooth fairy brought me a whole dollar!"

Gareth admired the gap in Maggie's teeth, then lifted an eyebrow in Gwyn's direction. "And to think I used to be happy with ten pence."

Nicholas tugged on a pant leg. "What's ten pence?"

"It's like a dime in Canada," Katie said. "Isn't it, Gareth?"

"Very good, Katie. How do you know that?"

"We learned it in school last year, after you came to live with us. Madame Morin taught my class about Wales because so many of the kids were asking questions about you."

"Pence is a funny word." Nicholas wrinkled his nose, then shrugged and turned his mind to more urgent matters, tugging on Gareth's pant leg again. "So what did you bring us this time? Did you get me the baby crocodile I asked for?"

Gareth smothered a laugh. "Sorry, buddy, no crocodiles. I heard they don't make very good housepets, so I brought you something else instead. Come help me unpack, and we'll see what we can find."

Rubber-gloved hands on hips, Gwyn sighed as she watched her family trek down the hallway toward her and Gareth's bedroom, with Nicholas racing ahead and Maggie and Katie each attached to one of Gareth's hands. Gareth looked over his shoulder when they reached the doorway, and she shook her head at him, trying—and failing, she felt certain—to look severe.

"You're spoiling them," she said.

"Only a little." He grinned at her, then disappeared into the room amid excited questions and shared tidbits from the time he'd been away.

Gwyn leaned a shoulder against the door frame and let herself bask in the sheer contentment of the moment. Gareth Connor—*her* Gareth, against all odds and probability—home again, reaffirming his place in their family, their hearts, their lives. He'd been with them almost nine months now, and she still felt the urge to pinch herself whenever he walked through the door. Who would have ever thought her life would take such a turn?

With a happy sigh, she turned back into the bathroom. Just the tub to rinse and the toilet to scrub, and then she could take a shower. After that, dinner, an evening walk with the kids, and then time for her and Gareth...

And that rain check.

Chapter 2

"Did you at least *see* a crocodile?" Nicholas demanded, gnashing his teeth and chasing his twin sister around the bedroom. "Did it have big teeth? Did it eat anybody?"

Gareth rescued a squealing Maggie by patting the bed beside the suitcase he'd just opened. Then he put a hand atop Nicholas's head to slow the perpetual motion.

"No real-life crocodiles and no eaten-up people," he said, fishing with his free hand under a stack of clothing. "But I did find this for you."

He withdrew three gift bags and doled them out to the appropriate children according to their favorite colors: purple for Nicholas, green for Katie, and blue for Maggie. The tissue paper from Nicholas's bag tumbled to the floor.

"Sweet!" the boy exclaimed. "A whole *book* about crocodiles!"

Maggie set the tissue from her bag to one side. "I got one about birds!"

"It's about pelicans," Gareth told her, then quoted

from the famous limerick, "It's a wonderful bird, the pelican; its bill can hold more than its belly can."

Giggling, Maggie wrapped her arms around his neck and planted a kiss on his cheek. "I like birds. Thank you, Gareth."

"You're very welcome, little Magpie." Gareth looked over at Katie. "How about you, Katie? Do you like your book?"

Gwyn's oldest daughter looked up from reading the back cover of *Island of the Blue Dolphins* and nodded enthusiastically. "Dolphins are my favorite animal."

"This book is more about a girl than it is about dolphins, but I think you'll like it. You remind me of her. Strong and smart."

"You've read it?"

"It was one of my favorite books when I was growing up."

Katie looked impressed. "Wow, so it's a really old story. Cool! And thank you!"

Gareth managed to transform a choke into a cough of sorts. There was nothing like kids to keep a man humble, even in his line of work. "You're welcome," he replied. "What about you, Nicholas?"

Nicholas, now sprawled on the floor mat at the foot of the bed, turned another page in his book. "What?"

Katie nudged him with her toe. "You're supposed to say thank you, Nicky."

"Oh. Right." Nicholas jumped up and wrapped his arms around Gareth's waist. "Thanks, Gareth! You're the best!"

"You're welcome." Gareth ruffled the blond head.

"Now, how about we head down and get a start on making dinner for your mum? Does anyone know what's on the menu?"

"Hamburgers!" Maggie beamed. "Your favorite."

Books in hand, the three kids trooped noisily down the stairs ahead of him. He paused for a moment before following, listening to the swish of water in the tub as Gwyn finished cleaning, the thunder of footsteps along the hallway to the kitchen, the lively jabber of children's voices. The comfortable sounds of a home. He smiled as the demands of the last three weeks of filming fall away.

It was good to be back.

A small, oblong, wrapped package dropped onto the duvet in front of the book propped against Gwyn's knees. She stared at it for a second, then frowned up at a bathrobe-clad Gareth.

"We've had this discussion," she said. "Presents for the kids are bad enough, but—"

Gareth cut her off with a kiss, then stretched out on the bed beside her, propping his head up on one hand. His eyes crinkled at the sides in amusement. "Can you at least open it before you lecture me? I think you might actually like it."

"That's not the point. I like everything you give me, but I keep telling you I don't need—"

He laid a finger across her lips and heaved a sigh. "Just open it, will you?"

Gwyn hesitated. She wished she could get through

to him how uncomfortable it made her to have him spend money on them this way. Try as she might, she hadn't been able to avoid the supermarket tabloid headlines that had persisted since the paparazzi had discovered their relationship. Gareth could tell her as often as he liked to ignore the hints at—and downright accusations of—gold-digging on her part, but they still stung. A lot. And she couldn't help but worry he might start to believe them.

Gareth nudged her elbow. "Well?"

She shook her head and leaned over to kiss his cheek, smooth and freshly shaved on her behalf. Her pulse quickened at knowing why, and it took major willpower not to toss aside the package in favor of unwrapping something else entirely. Leaning back against the pillows again, she tugged at one end of the ribbon tying shut the box and removed the lid.

"Oh, Gareth..." She lifted a gold chain from its layers of tissue and held it up. A shell-shaped pendant twirled from its end. "It's beautiful."

He nudged her again. "Open it."

She noticed the hinges at the top of the shell. A locket. She set aside the box and pried gently at the shell's clasp. It opened to reveal a picture of Gareth and the kids, taken in a photo booth during their vacation to Prince Edward Island. It had been the kids' first trip to the ocean, and not even five consecutive days of rain had been able to put a damper on their spirits. All four photo subjects wore the silliest of grimaces: Nicholas and Maggie had their tongues out and thumbs stuck in their ears with fingers spread wide; Katie's eyes were rolled back with her fingers pulling down the corners of her mouth; and Gareth had somehow managed to achieve a combination of all.

Gwyn burst out laughing at the incongruity of the photo in comparison to its finely crafted vessel.

Gareth grinned. "You like it."

"I love it."

"I had it made for you to commemorate our first family vacation. I picked it up on my way home from the airport today. So it doesn't really count as a travel gift, right?"

"Right," she said. "You win on this one. And I do love it, Gareth. This was my favorite photo from the entire time we spent there. I was so sad when we got home and I couldn't find it in the suitcase. Now I know why it went missing."

"But this makes up for it?"

"Definitely." Gwyn set box and locket on the nightstand along with her book, and then turned to face him. "It's perfect in every way. Thank you."

"You're welcome." Gareth rolled onto his back, tugging her with him into the crook of his arm so her head rested on his chest and his chin against her hair. The strong, steady beat of his heart thudded against her cheekbone. "So. We sign on the dotted line three weeks from today, future wife. Are you still up for it?"

"Are you?"

"I wouldn't miss it for the world," his voice rumbled beneath her ear.

She snuggled in closer, holding onto him fiercely, reveling in the feel of his hand slowly stroking her shoulder. She wouldn't miss it, either. She just wished the wedding didn't have to be such a production. But if it was what Gareth wanted, it seemed the least she could do. Especially after vetoing so many other things he wanted to do for her, such as the much-disputed housekeeper idea. As determined as she was to keep her life—and that of the kids—as normal as possible, he seemed equally determined to bring about changes he was convinced would make her life easier. It had been an interesting few months of negotiation with much discussion and not a few heated words, but with a little give and take, they'd managed to resolve most things. She'd won on the housekeeper issue, he'd won on having air conditioning installed in the house—

Said air conditioning hummed to life, sending a cool draft across the room in welcome respite from the late August heat. Gwyn smiled. Scratch that. Giving in on AC had been a definite win for all of them, making it the first year she and the kids hadn't had to move into the basement to escape summer's mugginess. That alone was worth giving in to Gareth's desire for a big fancy wedding.

The hand rubbing her shoulder slid down the length of her spine to her tailbone, then traveled up again in a long, soothing stroke. Gwyn's entire body relaxed into Gareth's, letting go of the weeks of life without him.

"Keep that up and you'll put me to sleep," she murmured.

"Oh?" Gareth asked. "Are you sure about that?"

The hand traveled down again, a little lower this

time, brushing over a buttock, tugging her nightshirt upward with it on its return. A flutter of anticipation danced in her belly. The hand returned a third time, sweeping even lower, skimming over bare skin, fingers slipping ever so slightly between her legs. Gwyn's lips parted on a sharp inhale. The hand retreated. She made a soft noise of objection.

"Unless, of course, you're tired." Gareth's voice held a note of amusement. "Because if you are..."

Her eyes snapped open and she glared at him. "You are a wicked, wicked tease, Gareth Connor."

"Oh, honey." He rolled over and pinned her beneath him, his hand going unerringly to the fire he had kindled. "You have no idea."

And he proceeded to demonstrate just how wicked he could be.

Chapter 3

"Mommy" —a small hand shook Gwyn's shoulder, jarring her from a warm cocoon of sleep— "Katie won't let us watch our cartoons!"

Gwyn pried open one eye and regarded her young son. Gareth stirred at her back. "Nicholas, what day is this?" she asked.

"Saturday, but—"

"And what is the rule on Saturday?"

"We're not s'posed to wake you up, but—"

"What *are* you supposed to do?"

Nicholas plucked sullenly at the duvet covering Gwyn. "Have breakfast and then watch TV until you get up."

"And is that what you've done?"

Her son's shoulders slumped. "No," he muttered. "But Katie burned the toast and I wasn't hungry enough to eat it."

A slight shaking of the bed betrayed Gareth's silent laughter behind Gwyn. She strived to keep her own face straight. "I see," she said. "How about you tell Katie I said to make fresh toast for you, and as soon as you've eaten that, you can turn on the TV. Will that do?"

"But we'll miss Spiderman!"

Gwyn glanced over her shoulder as Gareth's weight shifted, and she saw that he'd rolled up onto an elbow. He'd also tried for an expression of severity, but the upward twitch of his mouth and the way he avoided her gaze told her it was a thin veneer at best. She rolled her eyes and received a poke in her ribs in return. Gareth cleared his throat.

"Your mother has given you her decision, Nicholas," he said. "I suggest you leave before she changes her mind about the cartoons altogether."

Nicholas hesitated, his gaze going between them, weighing his chances of winning an argument against not one, but two adults. Then he heaved a mighty sigh and grumbled, "Oh, *man*."

Turning, he stomped out of the room, his bare feet slapping against the hardwood floor with a force that had to have stung. The door closed behind him, just shy of a slam, and his voice hollered, "Katie, Mommy says you have to make us new toast because the other stuff *sucked*!"

Gwyn sighed. If that didn't incite full scale warfare, she didn't know what would. She sent Gareth a rueful look as he gave in to the chuckle he'd been holding back.

"It never ends, does it?" he asked. Raised voices drifted through the bedroom floor from the kitchen below.

"Nope. Burned toast and Spiderman today, homework tomorrow, all-night parties before we know it. Having second thoughts about the fatherhood thing yet?"

His hand closed over hers as she made to push back the covers. "No second thoughts about anything," he assured her, dropping a kiss on her nose. "And if I remember correctly, it's my turn to play referee and your turn to sleep in."

"I wish. Celeste is coming over at ten to go over the wedding details, remember?" Gwyn grimaced at the thought of dealing with the wedding planner they'd hired. Celeste Dubois might be Ottawa's premiere event planner, but she was also pushy, highly opinionated, and far more interested in rubbing shoulders with Gareth than she was in listening to Gwyn, who doubted the coordinator would so much as notice if she didn't turn up.

Gareth frowned. "Speaking of second thoughts..."

Gwyn cleared her face. "No! Oh, lord, no. I'm not having second thoughts, I promise. There are just so many details to think about...I had no idea..."

"That's why we hired a planner, remember?" Gareth planted another kiss on her nose and then rolled away to stand up on his side of the bed. "I want you to enjoy your day without working yourself into exhaustion beforehand. This is a big event. Let Celeste worry about the details, and let *me* worry about the kids. Deal?"

Gwyn nodded. *Big event* was an understatement, in her opinion, but she supposed that's what she got for marrying a celebrity of Gareth's status. That, and the paparazzi that had started buzzing around again, and the bodyguard Gareth was trying to talk her into until things settled down. All of which seemed to diminish in importance as she watched her naked fiancé take clean boxer briefs and jeans from a dresser drawer.

Said fiancé glanced over his shoulder and raised an eyebrow. "See something you like?"

"Actually, yes." She met his gaze boldly, propping herself up against the pillows. "Very much."

Delicious anticipation thrilled through her as, jeans in hand, he started back toward the bed. A voice from downstairs stopped him in his tracks.

"Mommy! Katie's being mean!"

Gareth swore under his breath. "I'm really not going to be able to avoid that, am I?"

Gwyn's lips tilted upward, and she shook her head. "Sadly not."

He dropped the jeans onto the end of the bed and slid into the boxer briefs that molded themselves to his body as lovingly as Gwyn would have liked to do. She sighed.

"Very sadly," she added on a wistful note.

Gareth pulled on jeans that managed to look every bit as sexy as the boxers had, then returned to the dresser for a t-shirt, tugging it over his head as he came around the bed to give Gwyn a last lingering kiss. Feet thundered up the stairs outside the bedroom, and he pulled away, banked heat glowing in the depths of his gaze.

"Do me a favor," he whispered, "and hold that thought."

Chapter 4

"Gwynneth!" Celeste Dubois exclaimed in delight when Gwyn pulled open the door at ten a.m. precisely.

"Celeste," Gwyn replied, accepting the customary French Canadian greeting of a kiss on each cheek—or in the wedding planner's case, air-kisses accompanied by an exaggerated *mwah!* sound. She stepped back from the claw-like clutch on her shoulders. "Punctual as always."

"One has to be organized in my business," Celeste trilled. Daintily, she picked her way into the front entry, sidestepping a picnic basket and beach toys piled in front of the closet. "Doing a family outing today?"

"We thought we'd take the kids to—"

"A lovely idea! And such a nice day for it. As long as they stay out of our way for the meeting. We have a lot of details to go over. Your special day is coming up fast!" Celeste patted Gwyn's cheek. "Speaking of, we should get down to it. I hope the groom will be joining us?"

"Of course. He's in the kitchen getting some iced tea for—"

"Excellent. I'll just go through and say hello, shall I?"

Gwyn watched the petite brunette in the flirty floral sundress sashay down the hallway. She closed her eyes. Yup. There it was, just behind her temples. The subtle but unmistakable headache that accompanied every meeting with Celeste. She gave an inward sigh. Although, to be fair, Celeste wasn't the only trigger. The entire wedding was to blame.

A fairy tale come true, the tabloids were calling it. *The event of the year,* said the local newspapers, with more Hollywood personalities about to descend on the city over one weekend than had visited in all of Ottawa's history. Personalities Gwyn would have to meet, greet, and endure speculation from. Two hundred guests in total, along with a cake as tall as Katie, white-gloved waiters at one of the top venues in Ottawa, a bridal bouquet so large Gwyn wasn't sure she could carry it the full length of the aisle, and—

The sound of a throat being cleared penetrated her panic. Opening her eyes again, she turned to find Celeste Dubois' assistant on the porch, laden with so many things that it took a moment to locate the face among the objects.

"Carol!" Gwyn exclaimed. "I'm so sorry. I didn't see you there."

Carol Pal gave her a cheerful grin. "Not to worry. I'm used to working in Celeste's shadow. Is there somewhere I can set this stuff down?"

"Of course. Come in. Do you need a hand?"

The diminutive assistant staggered into the front hallway. "If you could just take the box off the top?"

Gwyn removed the most precariously balanced carton from Carol's load and pointed her in the direction of the living room. "Just set everything on the couch—the kids have gone to the park with our sitter, so I thought we'd sit in here where there's more room for Celeste's..."

She trailed off. While she and Carol had formed an almost instant rapport, Celeste was still Carol's boss. Dividing the poor woman's loyalties would be decidedly unkind. But unfazed, Carol grinned again.

"Celeste's theatrics?" she suggested. "Gotcha. And good call, because she's outdone herself this time."

She plunked down boxes, bags, a huge leather portfolio case, and a wooden easel onto the sofa, then stood back to survey the lot with a satisfied nod. "Good. I managed not to break anything."

Gwyn surrendered the box she'd carried in. "What *is* all this?"

"A wedding story." Carol's voice came back, muffled by the voluminous length of shiny voile fabric she'd pulled from the carton.

"A—what?"

Holding the fabric in one hand, Carol set up the easel with the other, spreading its legs with well-aimed kicks. "Celeste is trying out a new idea. A storyboard of your wedding."

"Um...why, exactly?" Gwyn watched the assistant drape the voile over the easel and secure it with a wide satin ribbon.

"To show you exactly how your day will proceed." Carol patted her arm as she passed by on her way back to the couch. "Believe it or not, most of her clients would *love* the idea."

Gwyn did believe it. But she wasn't one of those clients. She sighed, and Carol gave her a reassuring smile.

"Don't worry. I promise it will be painless, and it really is quite a lovely idea. Celeste was concerned that you were feeling a little overwhelmed, and she thought it would help if you could see everything all tied together before the actual day."

"Well, she was certainly right about the overwhelm," Gwyn muttered. "But I'm not sure this will help."

In fact, she was fairly certain it would have the exact opposite effect. So far, she'd managed to keep it together by *not* looking at the big picture. The very thought of seeing the entire day laid out before her this way made her stomach churn and her palms go clammy. She jumped as Carol's hands closed over hers and squeezed, gently but firmly.

"Breathe," the younger woman said. "You'll do fine. Everyone gets nervous before an event this size, but Celeste and I will make sure it goes off without a hitch. I promise. All you'll have to do is float through it like the princess you're supposed to be. This is *your* day, Gwyn—yours and Gareth's—and we will make sure it's everything you've ever dreamed it will be."

"Nerves?" Celeste chirped behind them, her heels clacking on the hardwood floor. "Perfectly understandable, *cherie*, but Carole" —despite speaking impeccable English, she gave her assistant's name its French pronunciation— "is right. We will take care of every detail for you. Come. Sit with your handsome fiancé, and let me show you."

Gareth came into the room behind the wedding planner, a tray laden with glasses of iced tea in his hands. His dark brows twitched together. "Everything okay?"

Gwyn took a deep, steadying breath. Celeste and Carol were both right. All she had to do was get through this. Let the two of them take care of the details, go with the flow, and survive the show. The most important thing was that she'd be marrying the man she loved—*how* that came about was secondary. Right? She made herself smile.

"Everything is fine," she said. And it was, as long as she focused on the brush of Gareth's lips across her cheek and the feel of his arm around her as they obeyed Celeste's urge to sit. As long as she nodded and oohed and aahed in all the right places as the planner proudly presented their dream wedding day to them. As long as she admired the bits and pieces that Carol pressed into her hands at the appropriate spots during the presentation—tiny samples of the bridesmaids' bouquets and groomsmen's boutonnières, scraps of fabric tied together in all the colors of the wedding palette.

As long as she didn't give in to the urge to bolt.

Mid-presentation, just as Celeste began the reception portion of her storyboard and Carol pressed a crisp linen napkin into Gwyn's hands, the front door slammed open and Maggie shrieked, "Mommy! Nicholas hurt himself! He's bleeding *bad!*"

Gareth was up and off the couch as fast as Gwyn, and they both arrived in the front entrance in the same instant. A tearful Maggie greeted them, pointing out the door to where Kristin climbed the porch stairs with a grinning Nicholas in arms, blood streaming from his forehead. Katie trailed behind with the mesh bag of sand toys.

"I fell off the slide," Nicholas announced cheerfully. "You should have seen how high I was!"

Gareth stepped out onto the porch to take the boy from Kristen, who puffed with the effort of lugging him several blocks.

"I don't think it's too deep," she said. "But I thought you should have a look."

Gwyn swept her son's hair out of the way. She dabbed at the gash on his forehead with the ivory linen napkin she held, ignoring a squeak of dismay from Celeste.

"Stitches?" Gareth asked.

"Cool!" Nicholas exclaimed.

"Is Nicholas going to die?" Maggie tugged at Gwyn's shirt.

"Nicholas is going to be fine, Maggie." With her free hand, Gwyn ruffled her youngest daughter's hair as her heart settled into its normal rhythm. Blood welled in Nicholas's cut again, and she firmly pressed the napkin against it, then glanced at Gareth. "And no, I don't think he needs stitches. The cut isn't very long, and like Kristin said, it's not deep. It's certainly not worth spending hours in Emergency. A butterfly closure will work just fine once it's cleaned up."

Kristin, who held a first-aid certificate and would be heading into her third year of university for nursing, nodded agreement. "That's what I thought. Here, let me take care of him for you. You're still in the middle of wedding stuff."

"Are you sure?" Gwyn asked, feeling her chance to escape slide away as Kristin's hand replaced hers on the napkin. "Maybe I should—"

"I'm positive. It's good practice for me." The babysitter took Nicholas back from Gareth. "Come on, Nicky. Let's get you cleaned up and bandaged, then we'll see if we can find a popsicle for you. Maggie and Katie, do you want to come with us or wait in the kitchen?"

Sniffling, Maggie turned water-filled blue eyes up to Gwyn. "Can I sit with you? I'll be quiet."

"Me, too?" Katie asked, her face bright with excitement as she peered into the living room at the storyboard and wedding samples. "We'll be good. We promise!"

Ignoring Celeste's smothered murmur of objection, Gwyn raised an eyebrow as she met Gareth's gaze. "Would you mind?"

"Of course not," Gareth's smile encompassed both girls, and his words warmed Gwyn all the way down to her toes. "It's their wedding, too."

Chapter 5

Gwyn closed the door behind the wedding coordinator and her assistant with a relieved sigh. She leaned against the wall and let her eyes drift shut against the throbbing behind them. She thought Celeste would never finish that storyboard thing. Seeing the entire event laid out like that, in all its minute, detailed glory, had made her feel more than ever like throwing up. Not quite the effect the wedding planner had been going for, she suspected, but then again, Gwyn wasn't quite the caliber of bride Celeste was accustomed to dealing with, either. She had never, even in her dreamy youth, wanted a big wedding. Not ever. Even now, just over a month out, she'd chuck the whole idea in a heartbeat if it was up to her.

But Angela, Gareth's agent, had been right all those months ago when she'd finally abandoned the idea of an L.A. wedding and presented Celeste, Ottawa's premiere event planner, as an alternative. It wasn't just up to Gwyn. Not when she was marrying one of the most visible men in the world. As much as she wanted to cling to the private life she and the kids led, and as much as Gareth assured her he would try to protect that life, the reality was that marrying him came with certain expectations. Certain changes.

Gwyn sighed. No, if she wanted to be with Gareth, she would have no choice but to make some concessions —starting with her wedding preferences.

A reluctant smile tugged at her mouth. Besides, sitting there on the couch with Gareth and her daughters, she'd felt distinctly outnumbered in her view of the proceedings. In fact, if she had to hazard a guess, she'd say Gareth had been almost as spellbound by the pageantry as Maggie and Katie had been. Heck, even Nicholas had joined them for a while, his round eyes speaking to his own enthrallment with the goings-on, especially when Carol had presented him with the dark blue velvet cushion he'd be carrying as ring bearer.

"Don't worry, Gareth," he'd said to his future stepfather, straightening his shoulders and holding cushion with a reverence new to Gwyn. "I promise I won't lose the rings."

"I have every faith in you," Gareth had responded, the twinkle in his eye belying the gravity of his voice.

The only hitch in the proceedings had come when Celeste produced a sketch of the church interior, pews filled with people, and began describing how Maggie, as flower girl, would lead the procession, strewing rose petals in their path. Maggie had pressed against Gwyn's side and looked up, her blue eyes shadowed with concern.

"I have to go first?" she asked. "By myself?"

"It's a very important job, Maggie," Celeste assured her brightly. "You'll lead the way for everyone, and all the guests will be watching you in your pretty dress. Isn't that exciting?"

Maggie's face had disappeared against Gwyn's ribcage. To her credit, Celeste adjusted quickly.

"How about this—you and Katie can walk together. Will that be better?"

But the little girl's head had shaken from side to side. "I want to be with you, Mommy."

Gwyn met Gareth's amused gaze across her daughters' heads.

"I don't see why not," he said, at which point Nicholas had demanded he be allowed to walk with Maggie and Gwyn as well, and poor Celeste's storyboard had required minor reconfiguring.

Still, as Carol had pointed out while packing up at the end, it was far better to find out these things now and avoid having one of the kids melt down on the day.

"Well?" Gareth's voice rumbled now near her ear, pulling her back to the present. "Are you going to survive the festivities?"

Gwyn opened her eyes and made herself smile past the headache. "Of course. It's a bit overwhelming, maybe, but I'll be fine."

"*Now* aren't you glad we hired a planner?" He tugged her away from her leaning post and planted a kiss on top of her head. "Can you imagine having to take care of all this yourself?"

She shuddered at the thought.

Gareth chuckled and then, his voice studiedly casual, said, "You do know that hiring a housekeeper would make just as much of a difference in your life."

"No housekeeper."

"The whole house could be clean all at the same time."

A little wistfully, she pushed away the appeal of that idea. "No."

"And you'd have more time for your work."

"We've had this conversation a hundred times, and the answer is still no."

"More time for the kids..."

She scowled. "Gareth, I said—"

"Not to mention more time for me," he murmured suggestively, nuzzling into her neck.

"That's cheating..." Gwyn croaked, inhaling his musky male warmth.

"I do my best." He trailed kisses along her collarbone.

"But the answer is still no."

"How about just until the wedding is over? So you don't have as much to worry about."

"Isn't that why you said we needed to hire Celeste?" she reminded him dryly.

"But when my parents are here—"

"I've looked after guests before, and I've survived. I'm sure your parents won't be any trouble."

He drew back with an aggrieved sigh and an eye roll. "You're a stubborn woman, Gwynneth Jacobs. My mother will adore you for that alone."

"Being stubborn?"

"She'll refer to it as not letting me have my own way all the time, but yes. Being stubborn. Now come and have dinner before the kids stage a riot. That storyboard thing took forever."

Chapter 6

"Well?" Sandy's voice demanded the instant Gwyn put the phone to her ear. "How did the meeting with the wedding planner from hell go?"

Gwyn glanced at Gareth, who stood beside her at the counter, doling out scrambled eggs onto breakfast plates. The raised eyebrow and twitch of his lips assured her he'd heard her friend. Injecting a note of enthusiasm into her voice, she tried to contain the damage Sandy tended to wreak.

"It went really well," she said. "Celeste put together this amazing storyboard thing, and she and Carol walked us through the whole day. They've put together a stunning event."

Gareth snorted beside her. Sandy snorted in her ear.

"Let me guess—you can't talk right now, can you?"

Hands settled on Gwyn's shoulders, and Gareth steered her past the kids at the table and toward the sliding doors that opened onto the back yard. Gwyn allowed herself to be pushed outside. She sagged onto the stone step and waited for the door to close again.

"I can now," she told Sandy, "and it was *awful*. Lord, Sandy, you should see what she has planned! I've never seen so many flowers or lights or that much sparkle in my whole life. And the cake! Don't even get me started on the cake. It's as tall as Maggie. And a chocolate fountain? Really? And ice sculptures. Who even *has* ice sculptures at a wedding? She seems intent on spending every penny Gareth has, I swear..."

And on the tirade went, running the gamut from linens to music—a string quartet for the dinner hour and a highly regarded local band for the dance—and everything in between, until Gwyn stopped mid-sentence, realizing how she must sound. She groaned, cradling her forehead in her free hand, elbow resting on her knees. "Lord, you must think I'm all kinds of ungrateful shrew."

"Actually, I was working out our alibi and wondering where we could bury Celeste's body," her friend returned with equanimity.

Gwyn burst into laughter—the all-consuming, belly-deep, spirit-cleansing kind that left her gasping for air and wiping tears from the corners of her eyes. "Oh, Sandy," she managed as she trailed off into chortles. "Thank you for that. You have no idea how much I needed a laugh right now."

"Anytime, my friend. Anytime. And the burial offer holds, too."

Gwyn giggled again. "Lord, I love you."

"And I love you back. Which is why I'd like to see you survive this thing. What can I do to help?"

"You've already done it by letting me vent. It really isn't as bad as I make it out to be."

Sandy made a rude noise.

"It isn't," Gwyn insisted. "The kids are so excited about everything, and you should see how pleased Gareth looked when Celeste ran that storyboard thing by us yesterday. I'm just being a grump about it all."

"Sheer overwhelm will do that to you. As will not having any control over your own wedding day."

"I'm marrying Gareth Connor," Gwyn reminded her friend. "*The* Gareth Connor. This isn't *my* wedding day, it's half the world's. People expect a show. Gareth's friends expect a show. I knew what I was getting into when he proposed."

"Bollocks. Those are Accursed Angela's words, not yours."

"Sandy! She's his agent. She has his best interests at heart, and—"

"She has her own best interests even more at heart," Sandy grumbled.

"*And* it's only one day," Gwyn continued as if she hadn't heard. "If this is what Gareth wants, then I'm happy to let him have it."

"*Is* it what he wants?"

Gwyn stared up at the maple tree overshadowing the back yard and grimaced. Was that a hit of crimson tingeing the leaves already? She wasn't ready to even think about autumn yet.

"Of course it is," she answered her friend." Otherwise he wouldn't have hired Celeste and approved all these arrangements. And seriously, what am I complaining about? I'm getting the kind of wedding every woman dreams about, and I hardly have to lift a finger for it. I should be grateful."

"You should be honest," her friend corrected. "But I suppose it's a little late for that, isn't it?"

"A little." A tap sounded on the glass door behind Gwyn and she turned to see Gareth pointing at his watch. She nodded understanding and gave a sigh. "Speaking of late, I have to run. I have the final fitting for the dress this morning."

"Ack! That's right, it's Wednesday today. I'm supposed to drive you over there! God, I'm the world's worst matron of honor, I swear."

"Relax." Gwyn stood up from the step. "I figured you'd be tied up with that project you have going, and it's only a fitting. I'm sure I can handle it on my own. Besides, Celeste's assistant is meeting me there, so I'll have a backup opinion if I need one."

"She's the nice one, right? Carol?"

"Celeste is nice enough, too, but yes, Carol is less...insistent."

"You mean pushy."

Gwyn chuckled. "You're right. I mean pushy."

"All right, but if you need me for anything, and I mean *anything*—a shoulder, a drinking buddy, a burial, whatever—you call me, got it?"

"Got it," Gwyn promised. "And, Sandy? Thank you."

Pushing the 'end call' button on the cordless receiver with one hand, she tugged open the sliding door with the other. Gareth looked up from wiping the table as she stepped inside. His mouth quirked upward in an amusement belied by the underlying concern in the dark eyes.

"Better?" he asked.

She set the phone on the counter and hugged him. "I'm fine. You worry too much."

Gareth abandoned the cloth on the table and slid his arms around her waist, leaning back to regard her. "You're sure? This isn't too much for you?"

She shook her head. "Every once in a while I get a little panicky, but as long as I remember to breathe, I'll be fine."

"I'm glad Sandy helps remind you of that."

"Me, too. She also offered to help me bury the body if Celeste gets too out of hand."

Gareth tipped back his head in a laugh. "Now *that* is a good friend."

"The best." Gwyn stood on tiptoe to kiss him. "I'll see you later?"

"We'll be home sometime after you, I suspect. The Children's Museum tends to suck up several hours, if I remember correctly, and Nicholas informs me that there's an outdoor section open during the summer, too. So...expect us for dinner, and enjoy your peace and quiet."

"Oh, believe me," she assured with heartfelt fervor and a grin, thinking about her planned post-fitting bubble bath, "I will."

"How did I let you rope me into this again?" Sean

asked, his voice dry as Nicholas swung off his arm and jabbered excitedly about the cool ship exhibit they just *had* to go and see.

Gareth shook his head at his cousin. "You know you're not fooling anyone with this pretend dislike for kids."

"I never said I dislike them. I just said I don't want any of my own."

"Or anyone else's."

Sean gave an exaggerated shudder. "Or that. Especially that."

"I might be more inclined to believe you if you weren't a school liaison officer and volunteering what, three nights a week as a basketball coach?"

"Two nights a week when I'm not on shift," Sean corrected. "And the liaison thing is about building healthy relationships between kids and cops. It's part of my job."

"That you volunteered to do."

"Just because I enjoy working with kids doesn't mean I should be raising them. Given my background, I'd be a crap father."

Gareth snorted. "On the contrary, given how you left your background behind you, I think you'd be a great father. Don't you agree, Maggie? Katie?" He looked down at the girls holding onto his hands in the museum ticket lineup.

Maggie turned a thoughtful blue gaze on Sean, then nodded. "I think so, too."

Katie tipped her head to one side. "Me, too. You should definitely get married and have kids, Uncle

Sean. Maybe you'll meet someone at Mommy and Gareth's wedding."

Sean turned a choke into a cough—barely—and sent Gareth a withering look. "I'm actually bringing a date to the wedding already, thanks, Katie."

Gareth gave an exaggerated groan. "Good lord, please tell me it's not Bunny."

"Her name was Carolyn," his cousin growled, "and no, it's not. It's someone from work."

"Let me guess. Someone safe, with no expectations?"

"Oh, for the love of—" Sean broke off with an eye roll and a sigh. "Look, Connor, I'm happy you're happy. Really I am. I think Gwyn and this crew" —he waved an encompassing hand at the kids— "are fantastic. I'll even admit that I was dead wrong about her in the beginning. But can we please, *please* stop wishing the same on me? Because believe me, cuz, it just ain't gonna happen."

"Next in line!" A ticket agent called. "*Le prochain!*"

Chapter 7

Lifting the heavy satin and tulle skirt, Grace stepped up onto the raised dais at the back of the bridal store and let the attendant—Sarah, if she remembered correctly—spread out the train behind her. She stared at her reflection, a tiny thrill of excitement thrumming along her veins. If there was one thing she loved about this whole affair—well, besides the fact that she was marrying Gareth...and that she'd finally be meeting his parents...and that her kids were having so much fun with it...

She made a face at the mirror. Fine. As blown-out-of-proportion as things had become, and in spite of her grumping to Sandy, she had to admit she looked forward to at least a few things. Having Gareth see her in this dress was one of them.

"Is everything all right?" Carol asked from her seat on the nearby sofa. "You're frowning."

Gwyn cleared her face. "It's fine," she said.

"You still like the dress?" The assistant coordinator's voice held a note of anxiety that said, *"Please please please tell me you still like the dress!"*

Gwyn laughed. "I love the dress, Carol. It's..."

Sarah gave the train a final fluff and stepped back. Gwyn pivoted her hips for a side view in the mirror, letting her gaze travel over her reflection's length. A wide, horizontal band of satin, reminiscent of a bygone era, stretched across the top of the ivory gown, resting just off the shoulders and beneath her collar bones. Beneath that, a fitted bodice hugged the curves of her body down to her waist, a row of tiny, satin-covered buttons securing it along one side. From there, yards and yards of more satin lay over a tulle underskirt, full without being unmanageable, ending in a mid-length train, with its only embellishment a partial overlay of additional tulle secured by a satin bow offset at the waist.

"It's exquisite." Gwyn finished, meeting Carol's gaze in the mirror.

"Fabulous. And the fit? It's comfortable?"

"It feels great."

A bespectacled, rotund older man joined her on the dais, a cloth measuring tape slung about his neck. Gwyn lifted her arms and allowed him to tug and poke at the fabric.

The man stepped back with a nod of satisfaction, his hands going up to hold the ends of the measuring tape.

"Is good," he proclaimed in a heavy accent she had vaguely identified as Eastern European at their first meeting. "Fit good. Look nice."

She reached impulsively to give his hand a squeeze. "Thank you very much. You did a wonderful job."

"Is job," he said with a shrug, but he looked pleased as he stepped down and disappeared into the store's nether regions again.

"Well, then. Hair is next." Carol gestured to the girl sitting cross-legged on the cream leather sofa beside her. "Brooke?"

The tall, slender girl untangled her denim-clad legs and stood. Celeste insisted she was a wizard with hair, but the electric blue, razor-cut tresses she sported—not to mention the full sleeves of tattoos that covered both arms—inspired a certain level of skepticism in Gwyn's mind. Still, she had no hair stylist of her own she could turn to, and so she really didn't have much choice. She stood quietly as Brooke lifted her hair first one way, then another, staring at the mirror as she did so.

"Your ends are split," the stylist accused.

"It's been a while—"

"I can fit you in tomorrow. Ten o'clock."

"Um..."

"Up or down?"

"Pardon?"

Brooke sighed. "Are you wearing your hair up or down for the wedding? With or without a veil?"

"Up, I suppose, and no veil."

The stylist twisted Gwyn's cascade of auburn curls up into a loose chignon and studied her a moment.

"Headpiece?"

"No."

"Flowers, then. Tucked into the hair. A braided French twist." Brooke, apparently a girl of few words, nodded satisfaction at her own decision. She dropped Gwyn's hair and stepped back. "Ten tomorrow."

Gwyn stared after the retreating blue hair as Brooke nodded to Carol, and sauntered toward the store front. A second later, the tinkle of a bell signaled her exit.

"Well," Gwyn said. "I can see why she and Celeste get along so well."

Carol smothered a laugh into a cough. "I know she's...eccentric, but she really is amazing at what she does. I promise you'll love it."

"And I can look forward to getting to know her better tomorrow, too. Oh, joy." Gwyn tugged up the skirt on the dress again and looked to Sarah, impatient to be gone. The bath she had planned suddenly held huge appeal—as did a mid-morning glass of wine. "Are we done?"

"Of course." Carol nodded to the attendant, and Sarah scurried forward to lift the dress's train again. "I'll wait here while you change, and then we can go over a couple of minor details Celeste asked me about. Is that all right?"

More details? Gwyn's head ached at the thought. "Fine," she said. "Whatever."

Back in the enormous, mirrored fitting room, she stood with one arm outstretched and the other holding up the dress bodice while the attendant undid the buttons running down the side. When Gwyn's hands were all that held up the dress, Sarah carefully lifted the satin skirt to untie the hooped tulle underskirt beneath. Then she let the hoops settle to the floor so Gwyn could step over and out of them.

"Almost done," Sarah said. She hung the hooped skirt on a hook along the wall and, smiling, met Gwyn's gaze in the mirror. "And may I just say again how very perfect this dress is for you, Ms. Jacobs? With the way your stylist has suggested you wear your hair, you'll look like a redheaded Grace Kelly."

Gwyn managed a wan smile in return. "Thank you, Sarah."

The attendant's look changed to one of sympathy, and she patted Gwyn's shoulder on her return. "Don't worry. All brides feel a little stressed at this point. Everything will turn out fine, I promise. How could it not, given who you're marrying?" She fussed around the dress, lowering the satin skirt back to the floor. Out in the store, the bell over the front door tinkled.

"Now, do you remember how we do this? Let everything drop straight down and then step out of it?"

"Yes." Gwyn took a deep breath. She relaxed her clutch on the dress bodice but didn't release it just yet. "And thank you. I know you're right about things turning out okay."

"Better than okay. I'll be there to get you into your dress so you look perfect, and with Celeste and Carol running the show, it will go off without a hitch. It really will be a Cinderella wedding," she promised. "Now let the dress—"

A shout from Carol cut her off. "Hey! You can't go back there! Damn it, stop!"

Sarah frowned and reached for the door knob. For a

split second, Gwyn froze. Then, in the space of a heartbeat, she knew. She spun around, clutching the dress to herself with one hand and reaching for Sarah with the other.

"Sarah, no! Don't—"

Too late. The attendant had already turned the self-locking handle. The door burst open, knocking her into the wall, and a camera flash blinded Gwyn. Once. Twice. Three times. Gwyn threw up a hand to shield her eyes.

"Smile for me, Gwyn, there's a girl!" a cheerful male voice said. "Let's have a look at that pretty dress of yours."

"Get out get out get out!" Carol's voice shrieked, accompanied by what sounded like repeated smacks.

"Ow! Easy does it, love," the man complained. "I have what I need. I'm leaving, already!"

Gwyn blinked past the spots in her vision to see the photographer ducking away from Carol's attack, backpeddling out of the fitting room. The event assistant chased him out into the store.

"I'm calling the cops, you son of a..."

Her voice faded, muffled by distance and the fabric of hundreds of dresses. Gwyn stood, stunned and disbelieving, unable to move if she'd tried. Unable to think. Somewhere, at the fringes of awareness, she registered Sarah standing up from where she'd fallen. Carol returning to the room. Both women touching her shoulders. Their concerned voices, their gentle hands.

Then it hit. The invasiveness of what had just happened. The sheer ugliness. A tremor began in her belly and spread outward until her entire body vibrated with shock.

Fury.

The satin against her skin turned from cool and smooth to something cold and repulsive. "Get me out of this thing," she grated. "Now."

Two pairs of hands took the dress from her and lowered it to the floor. Gwyn stepped away from it and grabbed for the tank top she'd left on a chair. She tugged the cotton over her head and thrust her hands through the arm holes, then picked up her capris and pulled those on, too.

"Gwyn, I'm so sorry," Carol began. "I tried to stop him. I didn't realize who he—"

"Don't." Gwyn picked up her handbag and headed for the fitting room door. "Just...don't."

She walked out, digging for her cell phone as she strode through the store. She didn't blame Carol—not even a little—but neither could she find the words to tell her so. Not right now. She thumbed the auto dial icon beside one of the names in her call list and put the phone to her ear. Right now, she needed to get out of here. To talk. And to have—

"Hello?" Sandy's voice answered.

"Meet me for lunch. I'm buying." Gwyn pushed through the door and stepped out into the mid-morning heat of the parking lot. She pulled the car keys from the side pocket of her bag.

"Um...all right. What time?"

"Now."

"Now? But it's only ten thir—"

"Now, Sandy." Gwyn pressed the button on the key fob to unlock her car. "Please."

Her friend's voice sharpened. "What happened? Where are you? Do you need me to come get you?"

"I'm fine. For now." Gwyn slid into the sedan and set her handbag on the passenger seat beside her. Closing her eyes, she rested her forehead on the steering wheel. "But you may need to drive me home after lunch."

Chapter 8

"Gwyn, enough is enough. You need to tell him how you feel."

Gwyn sank further into the dark corner of the pub where she and Sandy had met. She lifted her gaze from the coffee she'd ordered in lieu of the drink she'd wanted, having decided on the drive over that alcohol might not be the most appropriate solution after all.

"Tell him what?" she asked her friend. "That I'm dreading what's supposed to be one of the happiest days in my life? That I want all of this"—she waved her hand in a vague gesture over her head—"to just go away? We're just over three weeks out, Sandy. Gareth's parents arrive the day after tomorrow, we have two hundred people flying in from all over the world, and he's already spent a king's ransom on the event. What am I supposed to say?" She waved her hand again. "I've changed my mind? Cancel the whole thing?"

Sandy scraped a handful of bright red hair back and cradled her forehead in one hand, elbow resting on the table. "You should have spoken up at the beginning.

This is your wedding, too, you know. If you'd told him how you felt, that you wanted something small—"

"Sandy."

Her friend sighed. "I know, I know. I'm not helping. But damn it, Gwyn, I hate seeing you so miserable."

"I'm not miserable," Gwyn denied. Then she made a face. "At least, not entirely. There are still good things about it. I'm marrying the man I love, and the kids are all hugely excited about everything…and there's always the honeymoon to look forward to…"

"And you shouldn't have to try so hard to convince me. Or yourself." Sandy scowled. "I could throttle that Angela woman. She'll be at the wedding, right? So I can tell her what I think of her?"

Despite herself, Gwyn felt the corners of her lips twitch at the thought of stature-challenged Sandy going toe-to-toe with the svelte, L.A.-sophisticated Angela—and at the certainty poor Angela wouldn't stand a chance. But she shook her head.

"No, you can't tell her what you think of her. She was only doing her job."

"Making your life hell is her job?"

"Keeping Gareth's career on track is her job, and part of that is about public relations. His wedding is a huge deal for his fans, and that makes it a big deal for the studios. They're—"

"*His* wedding?" Sandy interrupted, her eyebrows disappearing into the bangs above them. "Don't you mean *our* wedding?"

"What?"

"You said *his* wedding is a huge deal, but it's not

just his, Gwyn, it's yours, too. Angela should never have put this kind of pressure on you. And Gareth shouldn't have let her."

"Gareth isn't to blame, I am. And I'm not even sure blame is the right word. What Angela said made sense to me at the time. It still makes sense."

"And you're still miserable."

Gwyn sighed. "Only because I'm being an idiot about the whole thing, I expect. I mean, really, what the heck is my problem? I'm being given every woman's dream of a fantasy wedding, and all I'm doing is complaining."

"Having the paparazzi pop into your dress fitting is hardly my idea of good time."

"Well, maybe not that part. But all the rest of it..."

Sandy leaned forward and took one of Gwyn's hands into both her own. "All the rest of it may be some other woman's fantasy, Gwyn, but it's not yours. You've been pushed into Angela and Celeste's idea of what this wedding should be."

"I haven't been pushed, really..." Gwyn demurred.

"Fine. Strongly guided, then." Sandy scowled. "However you phrase it doesn't change the fact you're not getting the wedding *you* want. The wedding you deserve. And as much as I like Gareth, I still think he should have seen what was happening and stood up for you more."

"You forget I'm perfectly capable of standing up for myself."

Sandy released Gwyn's hand and settled back in her seat with a mutter. "Capable, maybe, but you're way too nice to do so. I've half a mind to have a word with your fiancé myself. Surely that falls under my purview as matron of honor."

"It does not, and don't you dare. I'm a big girl, Sandra Masters, I can do this. Besides," Gwyn added hastily, seeing the stubbornness forming behind her friend's eyes and knowing she needed to head her off before she followed through on her idea, "Gareth more than stood up for me when it counted, remember?"

Sandy visibly tried to resist the distraction, but a reluctant grin crept across her face. "The prenup, you mean?"

Gwyn nodded. Sandy loved the story of how Angela had pulled out a hefty legal document over dessert and coffee at the engagement dinner she'd taken them out for. She'd slid it across the table toward Gwyn with a brisk, "I took the liberty of having this drawn up for you. Once you've had your own lawyer review it, you can sign it and send it back to me. Gareth can give you the address."

Gareth's hand had smacked down onto the paper before Gwyn could reach for it or read more than the words *Prenuptial Agreement* typed officiously across the top. He'd picked it up, stared at it a moment, then set it down in front of Angela. "Thank you, but we won't be needing this."

"But, Gareth—" Angela had begun.

"I said no."

Gwyn had put her hand on his thigh beneath the table. "I don't mind," she'd told him. "And it makes sense that you should have this. To protect you."

Gareth had covered her hand with his and looked into her eyes. "Protect me from what? You? I've already told you, I'm in this for the long run, Gwyn. I don't need protection."

"Things go wrong in life, Gareth." Across the table, Angela's voice had gentled, but it remained insistent. "Relationships go wrong. It's my job to look out for you."

Gareth had opened his mouth to speak, then closed it again, looking grim. He'd released Gwyn's hand, reached over, and torn off the top sheet of paper. With Angela watching in open-mouthed shock and Gwyn too surprised to object, he'd borrowed a pen from a passing waiter, stricken out the printed side of the page, and flipped it over. For a moment, the only sound between the three of them had been the scratch of the pen. Then he'd pushed what he'd written to the center.

"You want a prenup?" he'd asked. "There it is."

The bold, clear strokes had been readable from any angle, making Angela catch her breath and Gwyn's heart swell to bursting even before Gareth's fingers had found hers again, twining with them and squeezing tightly.

Prenuptial Agreement, the words at the top said, followed by:

Let it be known that heart, soul, body, and wealth...
whatever is mine belongs also to Gwynneth Jacobs.
Always and forever.

His signature had been scrawled at the bottom, and

after several seconds dragged past, Angela had raised her gaze to his. "I can't convince you otherwise?"

"No."

In silence, Angela had picked up the remainder of her document and slid it back into her purse. "Well then," she'd said, "about the wedding coordinator. I'll get in touch with her for you tomorrow, shall I?"

And just like that, the matter had been settled.

"Damn, I wish I could have been there to see her face when he wrote that." Sandy's voice pulled Gwyn back to the present. She chortled. "She must have been fit to be tied. I would totally have it framed, if I were you. You kept it, right?"

Gwyn patted the handbag beside her on the bench seat. "I did. But no framing."

"Suit yourself." Sandy pulled out her cell phone and checked the time. She cocked her head to one side, studying Gwyn. "I really should get back to work soon. Do you think you're glued together enough to get yourself home?"

"Go. I'm fine now. Thank you for coming to my rescue."

"Pfft. That's what matrons of honor are for, right?" Sandy waved away Gwyn's words and began gathering her things: keys, phone, sunglasses, handbag. "I'm just sorry I wasn't there with you in the first place. That s.o.b. wouldn't have made it in the front door, let alone into the fitting room. You'll tell Gareth what happened?"

"He'd just worry if I did, so no. And I'll call Carol and make sure neither she nor Celeste say anything, either. I may give in on the bodyguard idea, though, at least for the kids. Something like this would traumatize them for life."

"Whereas you emerged unscathed," her friend observed dryly.

Gwyn pulled a face. "Touché."

Sandy stood up, leaned over, and gave her a hug. "It's just until the wedding, sweetie, and if you can put up with Celeste and Angela and this entire hullabaloo, Monsieur Armand will be a walk in the park."

Chapter 9

Gareth stopped in his tracks, pulling Gwyn to a halt beside him. The three kids ran ahead to the low wall running the length of the enclosure for international arrivals. Airport foot traffic flowed around them.

"You're willing to have a bodyguard," he said. "Just like that."

"I decided you were right, especially where the kids are concerned. They don't need another run-in with the paparazzi—the school incident last year was quite enough."

"And there's no other reason for your change of mind."

"Of course not."

"Gwyn."

Her gaze slid away from his. He put a hand up to her face, cupping her chin and lifting it.

"What happened?" he asked.

"Noth—"

"Gwynneth Jacobs," he growled, "what happened?"

She sighed. "A photographer," she said reluctantly.

"At the dress shop. But Carol got rid of him, and I'm fine. It just made me think you might be right about having someone with us between now and the wedding."

A slow burn began in Gareth's chest. "Your fitting was two days ago. Why didn't you tell me? Why didn't you call me when it happened?"

"Because you would have overreacted?" she suggested. "Like you are now?"

"Damn it, Gwyn—"

"Stop." She put a hand on his chest. "You were out with the kids and couldn't have done anything anyway. Nothing happened. I'm fine, and I'm giving in on the bodyguard idea, which is what you wanted in the first place. Can we please just let it go at that?"

He stared at her, jaw gritted, wrestling with the not-unpleasant desire to rip someone's head from their shoulders at the thought of Gwyn being accosted. Gwyn returned his gaze calmly.

"I'm fine," she repeated. "Really."

Gareth drew a long breath and released it. "I'll call Guy Armand when we get home," he said. "But, Gwyn—"

She placed her hand over his mouth. "This is the part where you let it go."

He pulled her hand away from him, but before he could continue, the doors from the international arrivals area slid open for the first passengers clearing customs. From his post at the half-wall, Nicholas bellowed, "Gareth! Gareth! They're here, Gareth!"

A dozen or more heads swivelled in their direction,

and a ripple of recognition swept through those waiting nearby. Anyone who might have wondered at Gareth's identity upon seeing him had just had it confirmed. He sighed as cell phone cameras began pointing in their direction.

"Your son makes it very hard to go anywhere when he announces my presence like that," he told Gwyn.

Her lips tilted. "He's a little unclear on the discretion thing," she agreed. "But there may be a solution."

"Duck tape?"

"Nothing quite that extreme." Gwyn chuckled, and then her gaze turned serious. Hesitant. "While we were waiting in the car for you, the kids asked if they could start calling you Daddy instead of Gareth after the wedding. I told them I would talk to you, and of course, you don't have to if you're not comfortable with the idea—I'm not trying to pressure you or—"

"Gwyn." Gareth managed only her name before having to swallow against the sudden lump in his throat. He looked over at the excited crew awaiting the arrival of their about-to-be step-grandparents. His family. His and Gwyn's. How had he ever gotten so lucky?

He rested his forehead against hers. Breathed through the swelling of sheer gratitude that filled him. Lifted his head again to gaze into his future wife's uncertainty.

"I would be honored," he said.

And then his parents stepped through the automatic sliding doors and a whole new level of chaos ensued.

"Gwyn, dear, let me help with that." Gareth's mother took the dishcloth from Gwyn's hands and shooed her away from the sink. "It's the least I can do after that lovely meal you just served us. You must be exhausted with all the planning and running around I'm sure you've had to do. Why don't you put your feet up for a bit, and I'll make us some tea?"

Gwyn smiled down at the comfortably curvy older woman, from whom Gareth certainly hadn't inherited his height. "I expect you're far more tired than I am, Alwen. I'm not the one dealing with jet lag."

Alwen flapped a hand at her words. "Steffan and I started changing our sleep schedule a week ago to get ready for this trip. I'm sure the neighbors thought us mad, but I didn't want to miss a moment of my time with my new grandchildren." She tipped her head to one side, studying Gwyn with bright blue eyes. "What has you smiling so prettily?"

"You have the loveliest accent—I was just enjoying listening to you."

"And here I was thinking the same of yours earlier." Alwen's laugh was as musical as her Welsh-accented voice.

"I suppose it's a matter of perspective," Gwyn agreed. She gave the older woman an impulsive hug. "I'm so happy you and Steffan were able to come."

Alwen's wet hand patted her forearm.

"As if we would miss our own son's wedding. Or the

chance to meet Amy and your bunch." Alwen's blue eyes became misty. "I was beginning to think I'd never have grandchildren, and now look at me. Four of them!"

She plunged her hands back into the sink. "Put that kettle on," she urged. "I'm sure we could all use a cuppa."

Gwyn moved to do her bidding, filling the kettle from the refrigerator's water dispenser and plugging it in. Alwen's presence in the kitchen felt comfortable, as if they'd worked side by side for years. She smiled at the sound of dishes rattling in the water. Truth be told, she felt as if she'd known both of Gareth's parents forever instead of having just met them. The kids had accepted them with unequivocal enthusiasm, delighted with their new grandparents and more than willing to call them Nain and Taid, the Welsh names for grandmother and grandfather. And the fact that Alwen and Steffan had volunteered to stay and run the household while Gwyn and Gareth were away on their honeymoon? That was just pure gold.

Taking cups down from the cupboard, Gwyn released a small sigh. Now if only the rest of this wedding experience could be so pleasant. Before her mind could venture too far along that particular path—again—the return of Gareth and his father provided a timely distraction.

"All tucked in?" she asked as Gareth kissed her cheek in passing.

"And probably asleep before we got to the bottom of the stairs." He added the sugar bowl and a container of milk to the tray she was preparing. "They've had an eventful couple of days."

She knew the feeling.

As if he'd read her mind, Gareth traced a finger along her jaw line. "So have you," he added. "How are you holding up?"

Gwyn pushed away the desire—ever-present these days, it seemed—to throw herself into his arms, burst into tears, and confess her panic. She smiled instead.

"Hanging in there," she said. "But I wouldn't say no to an early night."

"You can head upstairs anytime. It will give me a chance to catch up on all the gossip about people you've never heard of."

"After tea," she said. She shot a quick look over his shoulder to make sure Alwen and Steffan were out of earshot. Alwen had finished the dishes, and the two had moved into the sunken sitting room. She turned her attention back to Gareth. "Did you manage to get hold of Guy Armand?"

"He'll be here at eight tomorrow morning."

"He was free that soon?"

"He's cutting short his vacation. I made it worth his while."

"The poor man! We could have—"

"Waited?" Gareth's lips thinned. "No. We couldn't. I have no intention of worrying about you or the kids whenever you set foot outside the door. Guy is being well compensated, and it's only for a few weeks."

"A *few* weeks—I thought we agreed it would just be until the wedding."

"It would be a good idea to have him stick around while Mum and Dad are looking after things for us. Just in case."

It was Gwyn's turn to pull her mouth tight. She looked away, but Gareth tipped her chin up until she met his gaze again.

"What?" he asked.

She sighed, struggling to find the right words. Ones that wouldn't give away her increasingly dark feelings about the entire affair. "You're sure the press will back off once this is over, right? They'll finally leave us alone?"

"Maybe not right away," he admitted, "and maybe not always, but yes. For the most part, they will."

For a moment, she let herself wonder if things might have been different if they'd planned something smaller and quieter. If they hadn't fed the piranhas and stirred them into a feeding frenzy with this whole glamorous, fairy-tale approach. If she had been stronger and stood up to Gareth's agent and Celeste at the beginning, instead of letting everyone believe she was okay with this—or if she spoke up now...

"Gwyn, are you all right?"

"I'm fine," she said. She gathered herself, held out a hand to him, and summoned a smile past the ache in her heart, almost believing herself. "Come on. Your parents are waiting for us."

Chapter 10

Gwyn gave her grocery list a last once-over, and then, satisfied she'd collected everything, looked up and sideways at the giant of a man accompanying her. "I'm done," she said.

Her brand new bodyguard nodded but said nothing. Gwyn tightened her grip on the shopping cart handle. She made a u-turn in the canned goods aisle and headed for the front of the store, wondering how long it would take to become accustomed to having someone shadow her. A week? A month? Personally, she doubted she would ever get used to the silent, watchful presence.

"It's best to ignore me," Guy Armand had told her when she'd tried—and failed—to keep up a running conversation with him in the vehicle on the ten-minute drive to the store. *"Pretend I'm not here, and you'll adapt faster than you think."*

Except it wasn't that simple. First of all, it went against Gwyn's very nature to ignore someone dogging her every footstep, and second, at roughly six feet, four inches tall and two hundred and twenty pounds,

Armand would be a difficult man to ignore under any circumstances. She reached the checkout counter and began unloading the cart. As distracted as she was by Guy's presence, a part of her brain still managed to focus itself on that evening's dinner menu. With Alwen, Steffan, Sean, and Amy all there, it effectively doubled the number of mouths she had to feed—no, more like tripled, given they were all adults with far bigger appetites than her kids. Did she have enough ground beef for the barbecued hamburgers? Maybe she should have picked up extra potatoes for the salad. Wait. Was she supposed to feed Guy as well? Was that something you did for a bodyguard?

She turned to ask him, but her gaze landed on the magazine rack and she froze, staring in shock at the prominent, unmistakable photo of herself adorning the front pages of three separate tabloids. Hands clutching the bodice of her wedding gown, the greater part of one breast on display for the world to see, the words *Cinderella Exposed!* stamped in bold black above her head.

Mortification burned its way up from her toes to engulf her. Her surroundings receded in a rush that left her swaying on her feet. A hand clamped over her elbow, and Guy Armand's face swam into focus. His mouth moved in speech, but Gwyn couldn't hear it over the buzzing in her ears. Distantly, it occurred to her that she wasn't breathing. She should probably make that a priority...

She closed her eyes. Focused. Drew a thin, shaky breath. Another. A third. The world slammed back in on her in a jumble of noise: too-loud music from the store's hidden speakers, the screams of an unhappy child, the smell of roasting chicken from the deli counter. Guy's sharp voice.

"Ms. Jacobs!"

The cashier's impatient one.

"Madame, est-ce que je peux fini, s'il vous plaît?"

Can I finish, please?

Guy's voice again.

"Ms. Jacobs—Gwyn—are you all right? Do you need to sit down?"

Gwyn looked down and saw she still clutched the bag of potatoes. Cheeks scorching, she mumbled an apology and set it on the conveyor belt. The cashier rolled her eyes and rang it through.

"Do you want to leave?" Guy's gruff question told her he'd seen the photo, too. That it hadn't been a horrible figment of her imagination. "We can send someone back to finish the order."

She shook her head. Whispered, "No. No, I'm fine. Really. I'll just pay, and then we can get out of here."

Her bodyguard didn't appear convinced, but he stepped aside, and carefully averting her eyes from her image, Gwyn moved forward to where the cashier tapped bright green fingernails on the counter. The girl's gaze rested on Gwyn's face, slid past her to the tabloids in the rack, returned. Widened. The green fingernails stopped tapping. In slack-jawed silence broken only by the snap of her gum, she readied the machine for Gwyn's debit card, finished the transaction, and handed over the receipt. Then—finally, blindly—Gwyn made her much-needed escape, trusting Guy to pick up the grocery bags and follow.

"Well?" Gareth asked his mother. "What do you think of her?"

It was mid-afternoon, and the first chance he'd had to speak with his mother alone since she and his father had arrived the day before. Between dealing with kids and catching up on family news—and then the meeting with Guy Armand this morning—it had been an intense twenty-four hours. This, a few quiet moments, made for a welcome calm in the midst of the storm of excitement.

Alwen smiled over her shoulder as she put away the last of the lunch dishes. She'd insisted on washing up after sending Steffan and the kids to the neighborhood park with one of Armand's associates. Gwyn—in the company of Armand himself—had been dispatched to the grocery store with a list for their first all-inclusive family dinner, with Sean and Amy both in attendance as well.

"She's lovely," she said. "And the children, too. You've a fine family there, Gareth."

Despite the warmth of her words, however, her smile flickered just a little, and her gaze didn't quite meet his. Gareth frowned. He rested against the counter, his hands braced on either side.

"But?" he prompted.

His mother didn't immediately reply. Instead, she closed the cupboard door, then folded the tea towel and draped it over the oven handle. At last she faced him. She tucked a lock of gray hair into the twist from which it had escaped.

"We've always been honest," she began, "with one another, I mean."

"And I expect us to continue."

Alwen sighed. "Your father and I can't help but notice...the two of you—you and Gwyn—you're all right?"

Gareth frowned at the question. "Of course we are. What in the world makes you ask that?"

"Whenever talk of the wedding pops up, Gwyn becomes...quiet."

"Ah. That." He relaxed. "She's feeling a bit overwhelmed by everything, but she's fine."

His mother raised an eyebrow. "No bride is so overwhelmed that she won't talk about her own wedding, Gareth Connor. Every detail we've had so far has come from you and the children. Have you not noticed?"

Gareth's frown returned as he tried to think back over the conversations held since his parents' arrival. He hadn't noticed. "Has it?"

"She's mute on the topic." Alwen shook her head, frowning back at him. "It's not right. And that business with Mr. Armand this morning. The poor girl looked positively green around the gills."

That, he had definitely noticed. His mouth twisted. "An unfortunate part of marrying me, I'm afraid, but only temporary. Once the wedding is over—"

"*If* the wedding is over."

He stared at his mother, startled. "I beg your pardon?"

Alwen crossed her arms. "Gwyn has the look of a doe on the verge of bolting, and you're not paying attention to the signs."

Gareth shook his head. "I know you mean well, Mum, but I think you're reading far too much into this. There's a lot going on in Gwyn's life right now. Managing the wedding, having the kids home from school for the summer, working, meeting you and Dad for the first time. If she's quiet, it's because she's distracted...and probably tired. It would help if she'd let me hire a housekeeper."

"Have you asked her?"

"To hire a housekeeper? She refuses."

"Not that. Have you asked her how she is?"

"Of course."

"And what does she say?"

"She says she's fine, not that it's any of your business." A note of irritation crept into his voice. He loved his mother dearly, but really? "I believe her. Not that *that's* any of your business, either."

His mother crossed the kitchen to stand in front of him. Shaking her head, she reached up to pat his cheek. "Gareth, dear, a woman who is a fortnight away from marrying the man she loves had better be a great deal more than just fine. Ask again, and this time, listen with this" —she placed a hand over his heart— "instead of your head."

Down the hall, the front door slammed open.

Chapter 11

Gwyn heard Gareth come into the room behind her, but she didn't turn. Instead, she continued staring out the window at the maple tree. She'd come upstairs as soon as she'd walked in the door. Just left Guy and the groceries in the front hall, climbed the stairs, and closed the bedroom door. Ostensibly it had been to give herself time to recover before facing Gareth and Alwen and Steffan, but she'd been standing here for at least five minutes without managing a single thought beyond noticing she'd been right, there was definitely a tinge of crimson in the leaves.

"I'm sorry, Gwyn." Gareth's voice was rough. Quiet.

She flinched at the sound of a paper dropping onto the bed. So Guy had told him. Shown him. She supposed it was just as well, because she wasn't sure she could have done so herself. Couldn't have described the photo, couldn't have relived the mortification of seeing it again. Not that the image would ever leave her memory.

Her toes curled against the floor.

"Why didn't you tell me they'd taken the photo?"

She shrugged, a tiny upward twitch of her shoulders. "I didn't want to worry you."

"I'm marrying you, Gwyn. That makes it my job to worry about you."

"And I'm marrying you," she countered, "which makes it *my* job to put up with things like paparazzi. I knew that going in, Gareth. I just—"

She broke off and clamped her teeth over her bottom lip.

"You just what?" Gareth's voice invited her to continue. She shook her head, blinking back a shimmer of tears. His footsteps crossed the room. Strong, warm arms encircled her from behind. He lowered his head to rest his chin on her shoulder.

"I hadn't expected it to be quite like this," she whispered.

"You're not just talking about the paparazzi, are you?"

She gripped his forearms, holding tight, not answering.

"Gwyn."

"I'm—"

"Please don't say you're fine again, love, because we both know that's not true." He sighed, his breath stirring her hair. "Tell me what's wrong. Please."

Downstairs, the doorbell rang. Sean and Amy arriving, no doubt. They should go down...

But Gareth didn't react, and she couldn't bring herself to step away from his solidity. Not yet. She thought again about Sandy's suggestion she come clean regarding her reservations about the wedding. Then she sighed. No. She really had left it too late. They could do nothing short of canceling it at this point—a solution that was out of the question...

Wasn't it?

She gave herself a mental shake. Of course it was out of the question. She loved Gareth, and she wanted nothing more than to marry him, and she'd be damned if she'd let the paparazzi change that. Or Celeste, or Angela, or anyone else. She was stronger than that. She could do this. She *had* to do this.

"It's nothing," she told Gareth. "Pre-wedding jitters, that's all. And the photo didn't help. Do you realize the whole world has seen my dress before you?" She attempted a laugh, but tears welled in her eyes, seriously undermining her illusion of strength and making her sniffle instead.

Gareth's arms tightened. "It doesn't matter. You'll still take away my breath when you walk down that aisle, I promise. How can you not? You already take it away every single day."

The tears rolled down her cheeks.

"It's not just the dress, is it?" he asked. He turned her in his arms. "Something's wrong, and I haven't been paying attention. Now I am. So talk to me."

She hesitated.

"Gwyn."

The sound of her name, spoken with such love in that rough velvet voice, proved her undoing. She buried her face against his shoulder, clinging to handfuls of his shirt.

"It's all of it," she admitted, hating that she could no longer hold it in. That she wasn't strong enough. And that she couldn't seem to stop talking now that she'd started. "I know this wedding is important to you, and I know I shouldn't be complaining, and I know Celeste and Carol have thought of everything down to the last detail, and that it will be utterly gorgeous, and I won't have had to make so much as a single phone call for any of it...I *know* all that, but it's still just so *much*. The flowers, the cake, the dinner, the venue, the press, *so* many people, two separate bands—sorry, one string quartet and one band—and I've tried to like it, I really have, but..."

"But you don't like it."

Tears streamed freely now. "I sound like such a spoiled brat. After all you've done, all you've given me... I keep telling Sandy that any woman in her right mind would be thrilled with all of this."

Gareth cradled her face and rested his forehead against hers. "But you're not just any woman, remember? You've never *been* just any woman. You're my Gwynneth with two n's...and you're entitled to have the wedding day *you* want."

"But—"

"And *I* am entitled to see that you get it."

"But—"

"Especially" —he put a finger across her lips— "when I don't give two figs about who attends our wedding, or what color scheme we have, or whether the flowers on the cake match your bouquet. None of it matters, because none of it changes why we're doing this, why we're getting married. I love you, Gwynneth Jacobs, and I want to spend the rest of my life with you. The fact you feel the same about me leaves me in a constant state of awe and wonder. You could turn up for our wedding dressed in a potato sack, carrying a bunch of wilted daisies, and I doubt I would even notice, because all that matters to me is the you inside the dress. You, Gwyn. I love *you*."

More tears threatened. Gwyn blinked fast, trying to hold them at bay. "But I thought you wanted a big wedding. All your friends…the studios…Angela…I thought it was important to you."

"And I thought it was important to *you*. I wanted you to have it all, so you could believe in fairy tales again."

She sniffled again, most inelegantly. "I *hate* big weddings," she said, and then she gave up pretending to fight the tears.

Gareth wrapped her into his arms and held her close as she cried out months of stress, rubbing her back, tucking a wad of tissues into her hand. He pressed his lips against her hair, murmuring words she couldn't hear over her sobs but that somehow still helped. And then, when her tears slowed, he kissed her spiky-lashed eyelids, her forehead, her cheeks.

"Better?" He relieved her of the soggy wad of tissue and replaced it with fresh from the box on the nightstand.

Gwyn nodded, and drew back to blow her nose. "Better," she hiccupped. "And I'm so sorry, Gareth, really I am."

"So am I." He brushed the hair back from her face. "I knew something was wrong, but I thought it was just nerves. I should have asked."

"And I should have told you." She used a dry tissue to dab at the damp spot she'd created on the front of his shirt. "So now what?"

"We can elope."

She shook her head. "No. The kids would be devastated. They're so looking forward to being part of everything. You've seen Katie and Maggie admiring their dresses...and Nicholas practices carrying a cushion up and down the hall at least three times a day. We can't not have some kind of ceremony."

"Fine. Then we cancel the whole thing and start over."

She grimaced and blew her nose. "The paparazzi would have a field day with that, and they'd just be all over us again when they found out the new date. I don't think I can handle a repeat of *that*"—she flapped a hand at the tabloid he'd dropped on the bed— "six months or a year from now."

"And I don't think I can wait six months or a year," he said gruffly.

"Which leaves us with the original plan." Her shoulders sagged.

"Which neither of us wants."

"I don't think we have a choice." Gwyn took a deep breath, and with a determined effort, she straightened, injecting cheerfulness into her voice—or what she hoped would pass for cheerfulness. "Besides, just talking about it helped, I think. I'm okay now. I can—"

Once again Gareth placed a finger across her lips. "Stop," he said. "No more pretending. Not with each other. That's what got us into this mess in the first place, remember?"

She sighed and nodded. He lowered his hand.

"Besides, I have an idea. Let's move the wedding up."

"Up—you mean make earlier?" She gaped at him. "But we only have a month as it is—when—we can't plan a wedding in—"

Gareth silenced her with a lingering kiss. Then he swept the hair back from her face, cupped his hands along her jaw, and said with absolute conviction, "I'm going to marry you, Gwyn, and I'm going to give you the wedding *you* want, and the paparazzi are *not* going to find out about it. Are we clear?"

The last of the weight Gwyn had been carrying in her heart for the past several months lifted free.

"How?" she asked simply.

"We ask for help."

Chapter 12

Gwyn opened the door to Carol, who eyed her without speaking for a long moment.

"You're sure this is what you want to do," the coordinator said at last. "You really want to plan a whole new event. You want to give up the wedding Celeste put together."

Gwyn rested a shoulder against the door jamb and folded her hands together in front of her. "I'm positive. The question is, are *you* sure? If you collaborate with us on this, you'll most likely be out of a job."

"Honey, your future husband is paying me enough to do this that I'll be able to start my own company twice over," Carol assured her. "Which is something I've always wanted to do, I might add. So I'm not worried about me, I'm worried about you. Whatever we can pull together in less than two weeks won't be anything like what we already have planned. I can't live with myself if that means you'll have regrets."

Gwyn only just refraining from sweeping the coordinator into one of the giddy hugs she seemed intent on bestowing upon everyone within arms' reach today—

much to Steffan's discomfiture. "No regrets," she assured Carol with a smile.

Carol gave her crisp, sleeveless yellow shirt a brisk tug to straighten it. "That's what I wanted to hear. Now let's get this party started, shall we?"

Gwyn led the way down the hall to where the others had turned the dining room into wedding central, hauling out laptops to peruse Pinterest boards, poring over the stack of bridal magazines Celeste had insisted on dropping off to Gwyn, and compiling a list of ideas on the kids' easel chalkboard. Using the latter had been Nicholas's idea, and he still beamed from the praise heaped on him for it.

All looked up as they entered, and Gwyn made the necessary introductions between Carol and Gareth's parents while Sandy mixed up a fresh pitcher of iced tea, and Amy fetched another glass for the coordinator.

"Right," said Carol, when the explosion of activity settled down. "First things first. We need an officiant—"

"Done," Sean interrupted. "I know a police chaplain who lives right here in Aylmer. He's free that Saturday and would be delighted to help out."

"Excellent." Carol stroked a line across a paper on her clipboard. "Now what about a venue?"

Gwyn looked up at Gareth. Gareth looked down at Gwyn. Everyone waited. Gareth smiled his agreement to a suggestion Gwyn hadn't even needed to voice.

"I think here would be perfect," he said. "What better place than where I fell in love with you?"

Gwyn blushed and tried to wipe what she felt was a fairly sappy grin from her face. Judging by Sean's snort, however, she failed. Amy gave her cousin's shoulder a poke.

"Your turn is coming, you know," she told him. "One day you'll meet someone and fall in love and be just as silly about it as Dad is."

Sean roared with laughter, joined by all the adults save Amy, who blushed, and Gareth, who sighed.

"Somehow I don't think that was quite as helpful as you intended," he told his daughter, "but thank you. I think."

Carol rapped on the table for attention. "People, we have a lot of planning to do in a very short time," she reminded them. She raised an eyebrow at Gwyn. "Venue?"

"Here," said Gareth. "In the back yard."

Carol motioned toward the French doors at the far end of the kitchen. "May I?"

Gwyn separated herself from Gareth's warmth and led the way to the doors. Outside, the late afternoon sunlight slanted through the maple, lighting up the perennial gardens that ringed an expanse of lawn on the right hand side of the back yard. Carol stepped past her and down the wide sweep of stone stairs. She toured the yard, stopping at each corner to tip her head to one side and frown. At last she returned to join Gwyn.

"It will be tight," she said, "but we can fit a twenty-by-sixty tent. That will give us seating for a hundred and twenty at a sit-down dinner. Unless you want to do a buffet, in which case we can fit a hundred and fifty."

"We're thinking smaller," Gareth said. "Forty,

maybe fifty, depending on how many can change their travel plans."

"Twenty by forty feet, then." Carol made a note. "We can set up for both the ceremony and the dinner at the same time, then turn the ceremony end into a dance floor. If you want dancing?"

"Oh, I want dancing, all right." Gareth swept Gwyn into his arms and waltzed her around the kitchen, snugged close against his hips. "Lots and lots of dancing. Slow dancing."

Carol rolled her eyes as she stepped back into the house and Gareth spun Gwyn past her. "This is going to take a while, isn't it?"

A breathless Gwyn pulled free of her fiancé. "Sorry, Carol. We'll try to be more cooperative."

The wedding coordinator shook her head and then surprised her with a quick, hard hug. "Don't worry about it. We'll get it done. I'm just happy to see you smiling."

"Me, too," Gareth said. His dark gaze met Gwyn's, warm, happy, and fiercely loving. "Me, too."

Chapter 13

Gareth closed the door behind Sean and Amy, the last of their company to leave. From upstairs came the sound of the kids' excited chatter and the lower-pitched tones of his parents as bedtime rituals began. He smiled. Good. That would keep everyone occupied for at least a few minutes. Hands in his pockets, he strolled back toward the kitchen, where Gwyn cleared away the dinner dishes. She looked up at his entrance and smiled. Deep, warm satisfaction filled him.

This. This was how she was supposed to look before their wedding.

Radiant, glowing, almost bubbling over with happiness. He plucked the dish cloth from her fingers and tossed it onto the counter, then drew her into his arms.

"It's good to have you back," he said gruffly. "I missed you."

She didn't pretend not to understand. "It's good to *be* back."

"You're happy with what we came up with today?"

"My head is still spinning, but yes. I'm more than

happy." She drew back, her gaze searching his face. "Are you?"

"Very."

"You're sure. It won't be anywhere near as grand as—"

He stopped her with a kiss. "Here's a thought. How about we agree to be honest with one another? If there's something I don't like, I'll tell you, and if there's something you don't like, you'll tell me. And then we'll discuss it like the adults we're supposed to be, and we'll work something out. Does that sound doable?"

Gwyn's expression became thoughtful. "I don't know. It sounds awfully complicated, but I suppose we could give it a try. It *might* work."

Gareth chuckled, shaking his head. He pulled her close again. "Oh, what a mess we nearly landed ourselves in, Gwynneth my love. I hated seeing you so unhappy."

"I hated *being* that unhappy," she mumbled into his shoulder. "And I still can't believe we're doing this... changing everything. Celeste is going to pitch a total fit when she finds out."

"She'll have no reason to if I'm paying her in full."

Gwyn shook her head. "Trust me, it's not just about the money for Celeste, it's about the prestige of planning Gareth Connor's wedding. Losing that spotlight will *not* go over well."

"And my wedding—*our* wedding—should never have been about someone else's ego. Besides, we won't be making the call to her, remember? We'll be winging our way to sunny Jamaica for a whole, blissful week to ourselves. Just you, me, the beach, and the palm trees." He nuzzled into her neck, tasting her skin, inhaling the faint, lingering vanilla scent of her shampoo. The very thought of an entire week alone with her, no kids, no interruptions...

Gwyn cooperatively molded herself a little closer to him and lifted her arms to encircle his neck. "You know Sean is an absolute saint for volunteering to call her for us."

"He has his moments," Gareth agreed, then he chuckled. "Although personally, I think he's quite looking forward to it. He wasn't a big fan of hers from the beginning."

"You never told me that." Gwyn leaned back. "Here I thought I was the only one who had Celeste issues."

"I thought you had enough on your plate, and I didn't want to worry you...which brings us back to the whole being honest with each other idea."

"A concept that sounds better and better the more I think about it."

The sound of a throat being cleared came from the kitchen doorway. Gareth looked over Gwyn's head to his father. "Hey, Dad. Problems?"

Steffan, not a demonstrative man himself, looked everywhere but directly at them. "Young Nicky is telling your mother he's allowed two bedtime stories, but Maggie says otherwise. As both are equally convincing, I've been sent to confirm."

Gareth sighed and met Gwyn's dancing eyes. "He never gives up, does he?"

His fiancée shook her head. "Never."

"I'll take care of the matter, shall I?"

"He's all yours."

He gave her a last kiss, holding tight to the promised bliss of their upcoming honeymoon, and then headed past his father on his way to the stairs.

"Tea, Steffan?" he heard Gwyn offer behind him. "You must be ready for a cup after all the excitement today."

Dealing with Nicholas required little more than a stern look and the point of a finger to hustle the boy into bed, but Maggie was another story.

"What does make a giraffe mean?" she asked as Gareth leaned down for a hug.

"Um..." Gareth raised an eyebrow, at a loss. "I honestly have no idea. Where did you hear it?"

"Nain said it. She told Taid she didn't want to make a giraffe by letting Nicky have two stories."

Gareth nearly choked on his laughter, but managed to swallow it so he didn't offend the little girl. He waited a moment to be sure he had himself under control, then cleared his throat. "A gaffe, sweetheart, not a giraffe. A gaffe is a mistake."

"Oh." Maggie considered the explanation. She wrinkled her nose. "Nain and Taid talk funny."

"Want to know a secret? To them, *you're* the one who talks funny." He tapped the end of her nose.

Maggie frowned. "Really? But I talk like everyone else."

"In this country, perhaps, but Nain and Taid come from another country, remember? In Wales, everyone talks like they do."

"You come from Wales, and you don't talk like them."

"I do when I'm there. But when I'm here, I've learned to talk like you."

"So in Wales they speak another language?"

"They *have* another language called Welsh, but that's not what Nain and Taid are speaking with you. They just use some words that are different than the ones we're used to."

"Well, it sure *sounds* like another language." Maggie sighed. "It's very confusing."

Gareth swallowed another laugh. "You'll get used to it," he assured his step-daughter-to-be. "I promise. Now, off to sleep with you. We have a busy day ahead of us tomorrow."

"Gareth?"

His hand on the light switch, he looked over his shoulder. "Yes, love?"

"I'm glad we're not having as many people at our wedding. Too many people make me nervous."

"I'm glad, too, Maggie. Good night, now."

"Gareth?"

"Yes, sweetheart?"

"Thank you for letting us call you Daddy after we're married."

He returned to the bedside, sat down, and gave her the biggest hug he could without squeezing the air out of her. "Maggie, darling, thank *you* for asking," he said, the tightness in his throat making his voice husky. "Now, off to sleep with you. Sweet dreams."

"Sweet dreams to you, too."

Chapter 14

Carol breezed back into the house at eight the next morning, agenda tucked under one arm and a take-out coffee cup in the other hand.

"We do have coffee here, you know." Gwyn closed the door behind her.

"Oh, trust me, I'll drink yours, too." Carol divested herself of handbag, keys, and sunglasses, dropping the lot onto the hall bench. "But I've been up since five, and there was no way I was waiting that long."

She took a deep breath and met Gwyn's gaze squarely. "You're still sure this is what you want to do? No minds changed overnight?"

"No change."

"Excellent. Then here's what we have." Carol handed Gwyn the coffee cup and flipped open her clipboard. "The party rental company is coming at ten to view the site and measure for the tent. You can choose your dishes and linens at the same time. Sean's chaplain friend will be by this evening at six to go over the ceremony with you. I have a new florist lined up that can do bouquets and boutonnières for you, but we're limited in what kinds of flowers we can use—I have a list—and we have to put the order in by noon. Oh" —she looked up from her notes— "and no centerpieces. The best they can do is give us a bunch of flowers. We'll have to arrange them ourselves. We can order vases from the party rental."

Gwyn blinked at her. "It's only eight in the morning—on a Monday. How in the world did you manage to pull together this much already?"

"Apart from calling in every favor ever owed to me? It helps that your future husband is being so generous."

A pang went through Gwyn. "That's the one downside to this, isn't it? The money..."

Carol patted her arm and took back her coffee. "Honestly? It's less than it would be if we went ahead with Celeste's plan. Even losing your supplier deposits, you'll come out ahead. Way ahead."

"It was going to be that much?"

"More." Carol's face took on a sudden expression of panic. She shoved the cup back into Gwyn's hand again, then rifled through a sheaf of papers. "Hell, I almost forgot. The caterer. We need to have meal choices done by nine. Nothing as fancy as the Chateau, but—ah. Here it is." She tugged a paper free and presented it to Gwyn. "This is the menu. We've used him before, for smaller events, and he's a marvel. I couldn't believe he wasn't booked already. The gods are smiling on you, I swear. Now, there's chicken tenderloin braised in—"

"Carol?"

"Hm?"

"Would you maybe like to come in and sit down at the table?"

The coordinator's gaze lifted from the paper. She stared around herself, as if surprised to find they were still standing in the front hallway. "Oh. Yes, I suppose that would be a good idea, wouldn't it?"

Gwyn handed her coffee back to her for the second time and led the way to the kitchen. Nicholas, Maggie and Katie were all perched at the counter breakfast bar, and the aroma of blueberry pancakes wafted through the air, with Alwen cooking and Steffan keeping plates filled. Sandy, who had arrived with delighted squeals and massive bear hugs at seven a.m. sharp, had taken up residence beside Gareth at the dining room table, she with her laptop and Gareth with the guest list Carol had assigned before leaving the night before. Both looked up at their entrance, and Gareth waved the list aloft with a smile.

"Perfect timing," he said. "We've narrowed it down to forty-four. I'll make the calls this afternoon."

"I drafted a cancellation email this morning for the remainder." Carol tugged a paper from her clipboard. "If it meets your approval, I'll send it out the morning after the wedding."

"So—what's next?"

"The menu, apparently." Gwyn pulled out the chair on Gareth's other side, waving Carol to one opposite. "And then flowers. Then the tent people come at ten, and the chaplain is coming at six. Oh, and Carol, we've arranged for Amy's friend to come over this afternoon to discuss music, so you can cross that off your list, too."

"What can I do to help?" Gareth asked.

Carol whipped out another sheet of paper and plopped it onto the table before him. "If you can look after—"

"Um, Houston? We have a problem," said Sandy, staring at her computer screen. She turned the monitor around to face them. "Twenty days," she said. "That's how long it takes to get a wedding license in Quebec. No exceptions."

The kitchen went silent but for the faint sizzle of pancake batter in the skillet and the tick of the wall clock over the doorway.

"Well," said Carol at last.

"Blooming hell," muttered Steffan.

"Does this mean we're not getting married, Mommy?" Nicholas asked from his stool at the counter.

"Will we have to take our pretty dresses back?" Maggie's eyes filled with tears.

Carol tossed her clipboard down on the table with a thud. "It means nothing of the sort," she said firmly. "We just need to find another place, that's all. Somewhere that won't already be booked...on four days' notice..."

Once again, the silence of disappointment filled the room. Gwyn closed her eyes, knowing full well what everyone had to be thinking. She was thinking the same thing herself. *It's just a wedding, Gwyn. Just one day out of an entire lifetime. Surely you can—*

"I've got it!" Sandy yelped, leaping to her feet.

"Why didn't I think of it before? It'll be perfect, and I know it's not being used that weekend, and I'm sure Tristan will agree—hell, he'd be thrilled! Ecstatic! And there's more than enough room, and all kinds of stuff we can use for decorating, and—"

"Sandy." Gwyn stared at her best friend. "What on earth are you talking about?"

Sandy grinned down at her. "The Canterbury Theatre, Gwyn. Where you and Gareth met."

Gwyn's heart skipped. She looked up at the man beside her, warmth spreading through her as the smile spread across his face.

"The place where I *started* to fall in love with you," he said. "It's perfect."

"I'll make the call." Sandy scooped her cell phone off the table and headed for the door leading to the hallway. "I should be able to get the key from him this morning, Carol. Can the party rental people meet us there instead?"

"Already on it," Carol said, furiously typing a text message into her phone as Sandy disappeared from sight. "Gareth, that list" —she nodded at the paper she'd put on the table— "needs to be taken care of today. We need to move up the dates for the gift bags, cake, and suit rentals. You'll have to move up the fittings, too, and then call Sean to let him know when they'll be. Can you handle it?"

Gwyn reached for the sheet. "We can share the calls. I'll take—"

"No can do." Carol pocketed her phone. "As soon

as we finish with the venue, you and Sandy are tied up for the afternoon with a dress fitting."

"I thought I was done."

"Carol and I talked," Gareth said. "We thought you might like something different. Something with a little less trauma attached to it."

"But—"

"It was Gareth's idea," Carol interrupted. "And before you worry about the cost, I called the dress shop owner last night and explained the situation. She's agreed to a straight exchange, and to let you have something off the rack. The fitter is dropping everything else and has promised he'll have the alterations done by next Wednesday."

Gwyn swallowed against the lump in her throat, but it wouldn't budge. Wouldn't allow her voice past it. She buried her face against Gareth's neck.

"You're welcome," he said, pressing a kiss into her hair.

Carol cleared her throat. "I hate to sound like a taskmaster, but I really do need everyone to stay focused. Gwyn? Are you with me?"

Gwyn took a deep breath, swiped away the tears balanced on the ends of her lashes, and nodded. "I'm with you."

"Good. Now" —Carol turned to the three kids seated at the counter— "how fast can you girls be ready to go?"

Maggie and Katie looked at one another, then at Gwyn, then at Carol.

"Go where?" Katie asked.

"As I understand it, this is your wedding, too. It's about time you were more involved, don't you think? You can start by helping Mommy choose a new dress. We'll pick up Amy on our way."

The shocked quiet lasted approximately two-point-five seconds before being shattered by excited squeals. Blueberry pancakes forgotten, the two girls slid off their stools and bolted for the doorway in a race to get dressed, almost plowing over Sandy in their haste.

"What in heaven's name inspired that?" she asked.

"Dress shopping," Gwyn replied.

"Dress— " Puzzlement gave way to comprehension in Sandy's expression. "A new one? Because of—?"

"Because of the photo, yes. It was Gareth's idea. As was getting the kids involved, I suspect." Gwyn looked sideways at Gareth's satisfied smile.

Hands on hips, Sandy regarded Gareth narrowly. "All right, fine," she said at last. "You've redeemed yourself."

"Thank you," he said, his voice grave but his eyes twinkling. "I'm so glad I have your approval. And now, young Nicholas, you need to finish up and get dressed, too. We have work to do."

Nicholas, who'd slumped forlornly at the counter, sat up straight. "I get to help?"

"Of course. You didn't think you were getting off that easily, did you?"

Nicholas grabbed the last blueberry pancake from his plate, stuffed it into his mouth, and followed in his sisters' wake with a muffled, "Yippee!"

With Gareth chuckling beside her, Gwyn winced

and called after her son, "Wash your hands before you touch your clothes, Nicky! Blueberries stain!"

"I will!" his voice floated back.

"Well then," Carol said. "What about that theater, Sandy? Are we in?"

Sandy grinned from ear to ear. "We're in, we can use any of the props we'd like, and we have the entire week beforehand to set up."

Gwyn watched her matron of honor and the coordinator high-five one another, happiness swelling inside her until her face hurt from smiling and she was certain she would explode. Gareth pulled her close and rested his chin on her head.

"Happy?"

She tipped her head back to meet his gaze. "Beyond imagination."

Chapter 15

Gwyn stood back from the mirror in the dressing room, staring at her reflection. From cap sleeves and v-neckline, the ivory gown's gathered surplice bodice hugged her torso snugly, embellished by a single beaded appliqué at the waist. From there, folds of satin flared outward over their hooped underskirt, swaying gently with her every movement, her every breath.

It may not have been her first choice in wedding dresses, but it was perfect. And it was hers, and it hadn't been exposed to the world by the tabloids, and it had been so right to do the exchange. Just as it had been right to follow Carol's suggestion to do away with the professional hair and makeup, and the manicure Gwyn had been certain she'd chip before she'd left the salon in the first place.

"Just be you," the coordinator had told her with a smile. "Be the woman he fell in love with. That's all he wants. That's why he's here. Why *you're* here."

So Gwyn wore her hair down, in the tangle of auburn curls Gareth loved to touch, with a handful of tiny blossoms tucked into it. Her nails remained unpainted, and only a minimum of makeup had been applied. A touch of foundation, a sweep of blush, a coat of mascara, a dab of pale pink lip gloss. She looked like herself. Felt like herself.

No Cinderella could have been happier.

A tap sounded behind her and the door of the theater dressing room opened to admit Sandy, bouquet in hand. Her friend stopped short, her eyes taking in Gwyn and filling with tears.

"Oh, sweetie," she breathed. "You look beautiful."

Gwyn felt an ominous sting behind her eyes. "Don't you dare make me cry, Sandra Masters. It took three tries to get this mascara on without smudging it, and I'll be most unimpressed if I have to start over again."

"So will your groom be, I suspect." Sandy managed a misty smile, dabbing at her tears with a tissue she pulled from the bodice of her navy chiffon matron-of-honor dress. "He's already looking a little impatient."

Gwyn's heart swelled an impossible size more, pressing against her lungs. Had any woman ever been this happy?

Sandy tucked the tissue out of sight again and cleared her throat. "Well? Are you ready?"

"Just one last thing." Gwyn picked up the shell locket Gareth had given her. Without speaking, Sandy traded her for the bouquet she held, then looped the locket's chain around her neck and did up the clasp. The cool of the gold nestled just above the hollow of Gwyn's cleavage.

Sandy took back her bouquet and smiled her satisfaction. "Perfect," she said. "Absolutely perfect."

Maggie, Nicholas, and Katie all waited with Carol in the hallway outside the dressing rooms, looking their grown-up best in their wedding outfits. Nicholas had his blond hair slicked back and wore a black suit with blush-colored vest and tie, with an ivory rose boutonnière pinned to his lapel; Katie and Maggie were dressed in matching taffeta dresses the same color as their brother's vest, each carrying a smaller version of the bridesmaids' bouquets. All three faces lit up at the sight of Gwyn.

"You look beautiful, Mommy!" Katie exclaimed.

"Like a princess," Maggie added, slipping her hand into Gwyn's and pressing close. "In a fairy tale."

"Does that mean I get to be a prince?" Nicholas asked.

"Rings, Nicholas," Carol reminded him.

Nicholas leveled the velvet cushion he carried. "Oh, yeah."

"Good call, stitching them to that pillow," Sandy observed under her breath.

"Experience," Carol said. She gave Gwyn the once over and nodded. "Perfect. Absolutely perfect."

Gwyn laughed at the exact echo of Sandy's words from moments before. "Thank you," she said, giving the coordinator a heartfelt hug. "For everything."

Carol hugged her back. "It has truly been my pleasure, Gwyn." She dabbed at her eyes, smiled, and then handed over the bridal bouquet. "Now, let's go get you married, shall we?"

All took their agreed-upon places at the curtained opening to the foyer for their unorthodox entry. Katie first, followed by Sandy, and then Maggie and Nicholas flanking Gwyn. The opening strains of Pachelbel's *Canon in D* reached them. With a final smile, Carol swept back the velvet drape, and they began their walk to join the rest of their new family in front of the raised dais: Gareth and Sean dressed in identical black three-piece suits; Amy in a carbon copy of Sandy's navy chiffon.

Gwyn's gaze traveled the grand hallway briefly, taking in the guests filling the chairs that had been arranged for them; the swags of ribbon and flowers marking the ends of the rows; the stretch of red carpet running the length of the aisle. Overhead, the domed ceiling soared two stories high, its gilt and deep red paint lit by a massive crystal chandelier. Somehow, the tired, faded old theater had pulled itself together to give the impression of grandeur once again, surprising her with its beauty and making a corner of her heart smile. As a hodgepodge of architecture went, perhaps it wasn't such a bad building after all.

Then Gareth turned, his gaze meeting hers down the length of the aisle, warm, bold, and fiercely content. It drew her to him as surely as a lodestone, taking away her breath and making her forget all about their surroundings.

His fingers closed over hers the instant she reached his side, strong and gentle at the same time. A reflection of the man they belonged to. The man who would give himself to her today, as she would give herself to him. With his free hand, Gareth swept back her hair.

"You," he whispered, "look stunning."

Impulsively, Gwyn stood on tiptoe to kiss him. "So do you," she said.

"Ahem," said Sean on Gareth's other side. "I think you're supposed to wait until *after* the ceremony for that."

Gwyn blushed, their guests chuckled, and their officiant smiled.

"Nothing like a little enthusiasm to start a marriage off on the right foot," he assured her with a wink. He waited for the laughter to die down, and then looked out over the gathering. "Welcome," he said. "And thank you all for joining us today to witness the joining of Gwyn and Gareth and their two families."

Chapter 16

"Well, you've gone and done it now, cuz," Sean's voice drawled. "Made it official and everything."

Gareth looked sideways at Sean, then returned to watching the sparkle that was his wife. Gwyn, dancing with Nicholas, smiled across at him. "Your point being?" he asked.

"My point being that you done good." Sean clapped him on the shoulder. "Real good. She's one in a million, your Gwyn. You're a lucky man."

That drew Gareth's full attention. He narrowed his eyes. "That sounded suspiciously nice. Have you been drinking?"

Sean chuckled. "Can't. I'm on call, remember? Not so much as a sip of champagne for me tonight. Ginger ale all the way." He held up a glass of bubbly amber liquid. "And I meant what I said. The two of you are good together, Gareth, and I couldn't be happier for you. Really."

Gareth pulled his cousin into a hug. "Thank you," he said. "That means the world to me."

They separated again, and Sean joined him in

watching Gwyn and Nicholas, who had long since abandoned his tie. Gareth had no idea where, and doubted it would be found again. The thought made him smile.

"It looks good on you," Sean said.

"What does?"

"This fatherhood thing." Sean nodded toward Nicholas, and then to the three girls gathered off to the side of the dance floor—Amy, Katie, and Maggie. "It suits you. And you're good at it. I'm sorry I gave you such a hard time."

"Don't be. Making me question my motives wasn't necessarily a bad thing. If nothing else, it made sure I was certain I was doing the right thing." Gareth hesitated, slanting his cousin a glance. If he didn't know better, he'd have said that was a note of envy in Sean's voice. "Sean—"

Sean raised the index finger of the hand holding his glass and reached for the cell phone clipped to his waist. He glanced at the display. "Hold that thought," he said. "I'll be back in a second."

He turned away to set his glass on a table, put the phone to one ear, and covered the other with his free hand. A touch on Gareth's arm drew his attention around to his mother.

"Mum," he said, stooping to kiss her cheek. "Having fun?"

"It's a lovely do, dear. But you know how your father is around a crowd, and the little ones are long past their bedtime. Time to head for home, I think."

"Of course. I'll find Guy for you and let Gwyn know you're leaving."

Alwen nodded, then jutted her chin past him. "Is everything all right with Sean? He looks very serious."

"Work, I think." Gareth raised an eyebrow at his cousin as Sean replaced the phone in its clip and joined them. "You have to leave?"

"Sorry, yes. We have a domestic with weapons involved. The negotiator isn't getting anywhere with the guy, so it looks like we may have to go in the hard way. Will you say goodbye to Gwyn and the kids for me? And I'll see you on Monday morning, six a.m. sharp. Jamaica, here you come." Sean grinned and gave him another hug, then leaned over to hug Alwen, too. "Sweet dreams, Aunt Alwen. I'll come by next week to see how you're managing with the kids."

Sean loped away, weaving through the thinning crowd. Gareth caught back the "be careful" that hovered on his tongue, already too late to reach his cousin. With a sigh, he checked his watch. Past eleven. Definitely time to round up the younger set and see them on their way. He threaded his way between dancers to swing Nicholas up into his arms and take the boy's place opposite Gwyn.

"Nain says it's time," he said.

"But I'm not tired!" Nicholas objected. He promptly yawned, and Gareth chuckled.

"Of course you're not. But it's still time."

"Aww, man!" Nicholas heaved a sigh. "Are you coming home to tuck us in, Daddy?"

Gareth's heart gave a thud at the new title bestowed

on him the instant the ceremony ended—would he ever get over the thrill of hearing it? He looked to Gwyn.

"Would you mind?" she asked. "With us leaving the day after tomorrow..."

"I don't mind in the least." In fact, despite his anticipation of having Gwyn all to himself on a Jamaican beach, he quite understood her desire to hang out with the kids as much as possible before they left. Sean was right. Fatherhood did suit him. "I'll get Guy to drive Mum and Dad and the kids home while we say our goodbyes. Does that work?"

"Perfectly. I'll tell the girls."

With Nicholas slung over his shoulder, Gareth started across the dance floor, only to turn back. "I almost forgot. Sean was called in to work. He wanted me to say goodbye for him and tell you he'll see us on Monday morning, six sharp."

"Six a.m. on his day off." Gwyn shook her head and smiled. "He's a good man, your cousin."

Gwyn eased her feet out of her shoes and regarded her red, swollen flesh ruefully. The low-heeled pumps had felt so comfortable when she'd worn them around the house all week to break them in. Who knew they'd become such instruments of torture when she danced in them?

The bedroom door opened to admit Gareth, his suit jacket long since discarded. Warmth fluttered in her belly. Lord, he should have left it off from the start. There was something so sexy about a man in a vest and tie, with his shirtsleeves rolled up on his forearms, looking like he meant business...

Gareth chuckled, drawing her gaze up to his face. "And here I thought you'd be too tired," he teased, bypassing the hooped underskirt she'd dropped on the bedroom floor when they got home.

She'd thought she'd be too tired, too. Given that it was well past two a.m., she had reason to be. But she wasn't. In fact, she felt quite...energized. She stood and turned her back to him, lifting her hair. "Unbutton me, Mr. Connor?"

Hands cupped her waist, sliding over the satin of her gown.

"I could, Mrs. Connor," he murmured. He traced the line of tiny buttons running down her spine. "But it would take so long..."

His hands slid lower and began tugging the dress fabric upward, gathering it, holding it out of the way. Cool air encircled her legs. Gwyn shivered, her body thrumming in anticipation.

"Too long, I think," Gareth added. He trailed slow kisses down the side of her neck and across her shoulder. A single finger found the edge of her panties and slid beneath the elastic.

Gwyn arched against him.

His finger teased the elastic lower.

She groaned.

A cell phone rang, setting off a vibration against Gwyn's butt. She yipped in surprise and pulled away, muffling her mouth with one hand. Spinning to face

Gareth, she watched him extract his phone from his pocket.

"Seriously?" he muttered. He made to set it on the nightstand, then paused, looking at the display with a frown. His eyes lifted to Gwyn's. "It's the Ottawa Police," he said. He jabbed at the phone's face with his thumb. "Gareth Connor."

He listened to a voice that Gwyn could hear but not understand, his gaze never leaving hers, his face slowly going gray. Gwyn's heart plummeted to her toes. *Not Amy...please not Amy.*

"Where?" Gareth asked, his voice hoarse. He nodded. "Yes. Yes, I'll be there. I'm on my way."

He took the phone away from his ear and ended the call.

"It's Sean," he said. "He's been shot. They're taking him into surgery now."

Gwyn stared at him, trying to make sense of his words. To reconcile them with her last images of Sean. Sean laughing as he tossed Nicholas over his shoulder at the photo session. Sean waltzing with each of the girls in turn. Maggie first, then Katie, then Amy. Sean toasting them at dinner, his green eyes sparkling and his expression alight with pleasure at their happiness. Sean, his coat and tie discarded, leading the entire gathering in the jitterbug on the dance floor.

Sean...*shot?*

Think. Gwyn gave herself a mental shake. She drew a breath and flinched at a stab of pain beneath her ribs. Gareth. Gareth needed to get to the hospital, to be there for Sean. *They* needed to be there for him. She reached up to touch her husband's face.

Her husband.

"Tell your parents where we'll be," she said. Skirts held up, she sidestepped him and slid her feet into her gardening sandals, because she didn't stand a chance of forcing them back into her wedding shoes.

Her wedding.

She and Gareth were married. And Sean had been shot and Gareth hadn't moved.

"Tell your parents," she said again, her hand on his sleeve. "I'll let Monsieur Armand know what's happening and meet you in the car. And, Gareth?"

Dark eyes, hollow with shock and disbelief, lifted to hers.

"Sean is tough," she said. "He'll be okay."

Her new husband wrapped her in a fierce hug, his entire frame shuddering against hers. Then he pulled away and headed down the hall to wake Alwen and Steffan. Satin gown trailing behind her, Gwyn went downstairs to where Guy Armand kept watch over her family.

Their family. Hers and Gareth's.

A family that included Sean and would continue to do so.

Because the alternative was unthinkable.

The End

Keep reading for a sneak peek at the next book

FOREVER GRACE

An Ever After Romance

Available Now

Chapter 1

Grace Daniels grabbed the smoking skillet on the stove, only to drop it again with a gasp of pain. Would she *ever* learn that the damned handle got as hot as the pan? Four weeks of burning herself, along with the food, and still the lesson hadn't sunk in. She snatched up a tea towel and dragged the pan off the burner, then thrust her hand under the tap. Turning on the cold water, she grimaced at the crisp, smoking black mess on the stove. So much for tonight's fried potatoes with sausage dinner. She sighed. Canned ravioli it was. Again. If the kids didn't mutiny.

Glancing out the window overlooking the deck of the borrowed cottage, she did a quick head count. Joshua was still curled up in the chair hammock with his book. Lilliane and Sage were at the picnic table, practicing their letters in the late afternoon sun that filtered through the brilliant autumn leaves. That was three present and accounted for, and the fourth was due to wake up from her nap at any—

"Maaa-ma!" came a faint call from the rear of the cottage. "Mama mama mama maaa-ma!"

The thin knife that had taken up residence in Grace's heart twisted. She blinked back a prickle behind her eyes. An entire month of repeated encouragement, and Annabelle still hadn't grasped the *auntie* concept. While Grace understood the two-year-old's insistence on calling her "mama," every utterance of the word seemed to add to the pall hanging over them all.

"Maaa-ma!"

Dabbing her hand dry with the tea towel, Grace dug deep to find a smile. Then she dropped the towel onto the counter and turned to answer the summons. "Coming, punkin!" she called.

Seconds later, she opened the door to the bedroom she shared with Annabelle, and the toddler squealed in delight.

"Mama!" Annabelle held out the soiled diaper she had removed and announced, "Poop."

Grace swallowed a gag. "I see that."

She relieved Annabelle of the soiled cloth and wrapped it up so the mess was hidden. Then she regarded the beaming, curly-headed imp with a wry shake of the head. "So. Diaper pins just made it onto tomorrow's grocery list, did they?"

"Poop!" said Annabelle. "Peee-yew!"

"Peee-yew," Grace agreed. She dropped the diaper into a covered soaking pail, then returned to lift the toddler from the portable crib. With what she considered admirable expertise, considering the scant month she'd been on the job, she plopped Annabelle onto the vinyl-topped dresser that served as a change table, washed and re-diapered her, then set the little girl on the floor. Annabelle wobbled for a moment, then found her balance and toddled back to the crib.

"Bankie?"

Grace lifted the bunny-decorated blanket, mercifully unscathed by the poop incident—she still hadn't recovered from the baby's trauma the last time she'd had to launder the treasure—and passed it to the little girl. Annabelle grabbed it in a hug, nuzzling her face into its folds. She pointed a chubby finger at the crib again.

"Sussie?"

Grace followed her niece's point to the pacifier wedged in the corner. She shook her head. "No way, munchkin. Sussie stays in your bed, remember?"

Annabelle peered through the mesh side of her bed and waved. "Night-night, Sussie."

Then, still clutching her blanket, she headed for the hall. She paused in the doorway to look back at Grace.

"Fine Jossa?"

"Yes, you may find Joshua, but you leave your diaper on this time." Grace put on a stern face and repeated, "Diaper on."

"Dipe on," agreed Annabelle. She turned and headed down the hallway at an unsteady run. "Jossa! Jossa! I up, Jossa!"

Grace waited, listening for the sliding door and the voice of the big brother Annabelle so adored. At only ten years old, Joshua had proved mature beyond his years. Grace didn't know how she would have managed without his help and guidance as she'd taken over the little family. Hell, with the exception of Annabelle, who was too young to be affected, all of them were mature beyond their years. Far too much so, but that's what happened when—

The knife in her heart twisted again, cutting off the thought. No. No dwelling. She had things to do. Little people to look after, dinner to remake...

Her gaze dropped to the sheets in the portable crib and she wrinkled her nose.

And more laundry to do. Again.

She sighed, thinking wistfully of her other life. A life where she'd been a successful thirty-two-year-old business analyst who wore smart pantsuits and wholly impractical shoes instead of blue jeans and sneakers. Where she'd traveled all over the globe and had hotel laundry services instead of being tucked into the backwoods of Perth, Ontario, with a crotchety old washing machine that needed its rinse cycle reset three times before all the soap was gone.

Out in the living room, the sliding glass door to the deck opened.

"Jossa!" squealed Annabelle.

"Annabelly with the big round belly!" Joshua replied.

The little girl shrieked with laughter, and Grace smiled, picturing her nephew poking a finger at the toddler's belly button and grinning one of his rare, lopsided grins.

More giggles followed, and then Joshua called out, "Aunt Grace? I'm taking Annabelle onto the deck with me. Don't worry, it's warm enough, and I'll keep an eye on her."

"Thank you, Josh," Grace called back. "I'll have dinner ready soon."

The sliding door opened again, but this time it stayed open and Grace heard the screen pulled shut instead. Josh knew she liked to be able to hear them when Annabelle was outside. He was careful never to forget. None of them ever forgot. Not their manners, not their chores, not anything that was asked of them. Ever.

For the third time, the knife twisted in Grace's heart. Also for the third time, she pushed away the melancholy and turned to practicalities, because time for dwelling was a luxury she didn't have these days. Not while Julianne's children needed her. Leaning down, she moved Sussie out of the way, gathered up Annabelle's sheets, then trudged down the hallway to the mudroom off the kitchen, where the ancient washing machine resided. No dryer, but it was enough for now. As long as the kids stayed safe, that was all that mattered. All that Julianne had wanted.

Grace lifted the lid on the washer and stuffed the sheets in. Laundry, then dinner, then a movie, she decided, and tomorrow, a coveted trip into town with a stop for ice cream.

And a call to the hospital.

Sean McKittrick moved the driver's seat as far back as it would go and then, using both hands, maneuvered his plaster-encased leg past the car doorjamb. His foot landed with a thud in the gravel of the driveway, sending a jolt through the limb that traveled all the way up to his gritted teeth. He squeezed his eyes closed and waited for the breath to return to his lungs. Damn, he'd be glad when it stopped doing that at every little bump.

Three more weeks, he reminded himself. *Just three more weeks.*

Followed by a leg brace and months of physiotherapy, but hey, one hurdle at a time, right?

With the pain reduced again to its usual aching throb, he set his right foot beside the first and twisted around to reach the crutches he'd stowed in the back seat. A grunt and an almighty heave brought him to his feet, where he teetered for a precarious few seconds before finding his balance. Then, glumly, he regarded the sloping, uneven stretch of path between him and the cottage porch. Huh. Maybe it *was* as bad as he'd remembered. He sighed. Well, he was here now, and he couldn't very well sleep in the SUV. Nor could he manage the trip back to Ottawa today. He'd already skipped the last two doses of pain meds so he could drive up here in the first place. If he didn't get something more than ibuprofen into him soon, he'd be tempted to rip the damned leg off altogether and be done with it.

Besides, the peace and quiet of autumn here was exactly what he needed. No one dropping in to see how he was doing, and no noisy neighbors. Hell, no neighbors at all at this time of year. He surveyed the cottage with satisfaction, letting the stillness penetrate. Set about ten feet lower than the driveway and tucked beneath massive maples and pines, the little cedar-clad box wasn't much to look at, but it was watertight and comfortable.

He slammed the driver's door and crutched his way around to the rear hatch, his travels made more awkward than usual by the crutches sinking into the driveway's gravel. Just as he reached in for his duffel bag, the cell phone hanging from his belt rang. He unclipped it, glanced at the display, and grimaced. Yep. Right on time, as expected. He thumbed the button to answer.

"Hey," he said. "How's the happy honeymooner?"

"A little stunned to find his cousin has up and left town three weeks after being shot and having his leg put back together like a bloody jigsaw puzzle," a familiar and famous Welsh-accented voice retorted. "I thought we agreed you'd come and stay with us when we got back."

Sean snorted. "You and Gwyn agreed. I don't remember having any more say in that than I did the nurse idea."

"The nurse idea was the only way they would release you from hospital," Gareth Connor reminded him. "*And* the only way Gwyn agreed to leave you here alone in the first place."

"Yeah, well, I decided I'd recover faster at the cottage than I would at your place. No offense, cuz, but watching the two of you make post-honeymoon cow's eyes at one another for the next three weeks wasn't my idea of fun. And as cute as Gwyn's kids are..." Sean shuddered. "Not my idea of a peaceful convalescence."

"And being on your own out in the middle of

nowhere seemed like a better idea how? You're in a full leg cast and on crutches, Sean. What happens if you fall?"

"Then I imagine I'll figure out a way to get up. Look, I'm not planning to go on any hikes, Gareth. I'm just going to read and nap and hang out in the hammock on the back deck. I'll be fine."

"You could have at least taken the nurse with you."

"Are you nuts? Have Perky Pam at the cottage for three weeks with me? God, no." Sean shuddered again, remembering the cheerfully efficient private nurse Gareth had insisted on hiring for him. Nice enough. Cute, even. But the woman had never stopped talking. *Ever.* He shook his head. "I'd have had to kill her, and that's kind of frowned upon in my line of work."

"So is stupidity, I would think."

Sean eyed the path to the cottage once more, inclined to agree with Gareth but not about to tell him so. Especially when his gaze settled on what looked like awfully fresh bear scat just off the driveway. Great. Just freaking great.

"Gareth. I'm thirty-eight years old, I have my cell phone, and I'm a cop. If anything goes wrong, I'm pretty sure I can figure out what to do. Now, I know you're used to getting your own way, being a Hollywood star and all —"

"Screw off."

Sean grinned and continued as if he hadn't heard, "But if you don't mind, I'd like to get settled sometime before dark."

"You really are annoying sometimes."

"Back atcha, Connor."

Gareth's annoyed sigh echoed down the line. "Fine. Have it your way. But keep your cell phone on you at all times, and call me every couple of days so I at least know you're still alive."

"Anything else, *dad*?"

"Damn it, Sean—"

"I'm sorry," Sean interrupted. He needed to get off this damned leg before it collapsed under him. Time to stop needling his cousin. "I know you're worried, but I really am all right. They put the cast on yesterday, the incision has healed beautifully, and they said I handle the crutches like a pro. And yes, I'll call every few days. You have my word. In the meantime, say hi to Gwyn and the kids for me, all right?"

"I still don't like this," Gareth muttered. "But fine. Just look after yourself."

The connection went dead, and Sean slid the cell phone back into its clip on his belt. Then, the sweat of exertion already turning his shirt clammy, he took the duffel bag from beside the four bulging grocery sacks in the trunk, slung it across his back, and settled his crutches into his armpits for the first of several trips down the slope to the cottage.

Chapter 2

With Sage keeping Annabelle out from under foot, and Lilliane and Joshua helping to carry groceries, Grace had the minivan emptied in short order after their jaunt into Perth. Spirits and energies had remained high all the way back to the cottage, possibly due to the sugar rush of their final stop. The ice cream had been an enormous hit all around, especially with Annabelle, who had delighted in smearing the cold confection over most of her body.

Grace glanced into the living room and grinned at the sight of quiet little Sage patiently trying to wipe the toddler's sticky face as she sang, "This is the way we wash our face, wash our face, wash our face..."

"Aunt Grace?"

She looked down at Lilliane, whose arms strained under the bag of potatoes she carried. She shoved the cans of stew and ravioli she was holding onto the shelf, and relieved the eight-year-old of her load.

"Thank you, sweetie," she said, smoothing her free hand over her niece's dark hair. "You're an amazing helper. You, too, Josh."

Her nephew shrugged. "We're a family," he said, his voice quiet. "It's what we're supposed to do."

Grace forced a smile and reached past him to flick on the kitchen light switch. The early evening gloom retreated. "You're right. It *is* what we're supposed to do. And now *I'm* supposed to make dinner, which is already late, and *you* are supposed to go and find something fun to do until it's ready."

Josh and Lilliane exchanged a glance.

"Ravioli again?" Lilliane asked with studied casualness.

Grace laughed. "How about I take another shot at the sausages and fried potatoes? I promise not to burn them this time."

Another glance was exchanged.

"If you're sure..." said Josh.

She ruffled his hair playfully. "I'm sure, smarty pants. Now go, before I change my mind and put you to work peeling potatoes."

"Do you want me to do that for you? I can."

Grace held back a sigh. "I was only kidding. You've done enough today, Josh. Now go find something *you* want to do."

"Can I go next door to read?"

"Do you think you'll have enough light?"

"Sunset isn't for another half hour."

"All right. Just make sure you're listening for me when I call, and use the side door so Annabelle doesn't see you leave."

Joshua nodded agreement, picked up the book he'd left on the counter earlier, and slipped into the mudroom behind the kitchen. A few seconds later, Grace watched through the kitchen window as he disappeared along the path leading to the neighboring cottage, where he liked to go when he needed a break from all-female company.

Luc, her friend and lawyer who owned their cottage, had said his neighbor only put in an appearance during the summer months, so letting Josh hang out and read on the deck would be fine. She'd been a mess of nerves the first few times, hating that he was out of sight and reach, but now that their little family was settling into a routine, she'd begun to relax. It did Josh good to have the independence, and he was still near enough that he could hear her call to him.

And she could hear him if anything went wrong.

She opened the window a few inches, then turned and smiled at Lilliane. "You, too, kiddo. Go find something fun to do. You're officially off duty."

Too-serious brown eyes regarded her. "What about you, Aunt Grace? Are you ever off duty?"

Grace shrugged off thoughts of how bone-weary she was these days. She gave her niece a wink. "Didn't you know? That's what kids' bedtimes are for. And cartoons. In fact, why don't you put a cartoon on now? Something Annabelle likes, so she'll leave you alone for a while."

Lilliane rewarded her suggestion with a smile. "I'll put on *Snow White*. It's her favorite."

"Lovely," said Grace. Then, as her niece joined Annabelle and Sage in the next room, she took a paring knife from the drawer, slit open the bag of potatoes, and gritted her teeth in preparation for yet another onslaught of *Some Day My Prince Will Come*.

Sean came awake to the screech of a blue jay outside his bedroom window. He listened to its scolding for a few minutes, a grin on his face. Noisy, yes. But it still beat the hell out of being roused from a nap by Perky Pam's, "Wakey, wakey! If you keep sleeping now, you'll never sleep tonight, you know!"

And Gareth had wanted him to bring her along to the cottage? Ha. Not in a million years.

Sean stretched leisurely. By the time he'd finished hauling the groceries in from the SUV, turned himself into a pretzel in order to get the cottage's water supply back on, and finally been able to take the long-overdue painkillers, his leg had felt like someone had run it through a grinder. He was much relieved to find that sleep and medication had worked a small miracle to ease the discomfort.

First, because he really needed time to recuperate away from the well-meaning questions and concerns of so many. And second, having to admit to his cousin he'd made a mistake in coming here—or even worse, ask for a rescue—would *so* not have been cool. Gareth would have never let him live it down.

Flexing the foot of his injured leg, Sean gauged the pain level. Definitely better. Tolerable, even. And, judging by the deepening shadows in the bedroom, he'd slept a good three hours, which meant he could take another painkiller soon. He grinned again, feeling quite vindicated in his decision to make the trip out here. A couple of weeks of tranquility were exactly what he needed.

He levered himself upright, swung the cast off the bed, and reached for the crutches. In short order, he visited the facilities, took another capsule, and made himself a cup of tea in a spill-proof travel mug that he tucked into a pocket for transportation. He eyed the bottle of Scotch sitting on the counter as he passed by.

Soon, he promised himself. As soon as he was off the pills. Two days, maybe three, and he'd start cutting back. See if he couldn't wean himself off them by the end of next weekend, so he could at least enjoy a good, stiff drink—his first since the weekend before getting in the way of that damned bullet.

For now, however, tea, his hammock—if he could manage to get into the thing without killing himself—and a lakeside evening would do quite nicely.

He flicked off the kitchen light switch, then traveled across the living room to the sliding glass door onto the wooden deck. Thud, swing. Thud, swing. He grimaced. Damned if he wasn't getting the hang of this crutch thing. He flipped the lock on the door and slid it open, then maneuvered awkwardly through the gap—in time for a child's angry wail to shatter the early evening silence.

Sean's head shot up. He stared through the shadowed woods at the cottage next door, its partial outline visible through the leaves and gathering shadows. A *kid*? What in—

The scrape of a shoe against the deck caught his

ear. He swiveled, teetered, regained his balance. He gaped at the boy who had frozen, half out of Sean's hammock, eyes wide and terrified behind wire-framed glasses. For a long few seconds, neither of them moved. Sean recovered first, just as another screech echoed through the trees.

"Who the *hell* are you?" he snarled, thudding toward the boy. "And what in God's name is that racket?"

The boy bolted from the hammock and dived past him, headed for the stairs. Sean threw out an arm to stop him. His fingers brushed against a nylon jacket but closed on air. One crutch fell away to land with a hollow thump on the wooden deck. Sean struggled for balance as the boy's footsteps thundered down the stairs and onto the dirt path through the trees dividing the cottages. Sean's free arm pinwheeled madly. He tipped forward. Back. Further forward. Then, losing the battle, he pitched full length onto the deck floor, white-hot agony tearing through his thigh.

"Son of a goddamn *bitch*," he bellowed.

OTHER BOOKS BY LINDA POITEVIN

Gwynneth Ever After

Forever Grace

Always and Forever

Abigail Always

Shadow of Doubt

Writing as Lydia M. Hawke

Sins of the Angels

Sins of the Son

Sins of the Lost

Sins of the Warrior

About the Author

Like all romance writers, Linda Poitevin is a firm believer in happy-ever-afters, but she also knows how hard you have to work at relationships sometimes. She tries to reflect that in stories about people who live, laugh, cry, and love just as hard as they can in this crazy life we all share—people who are as real to her as she hopes they'll be to you.

Linda lives outside Ottawa, Canada's capital, where (in her other-than-writing life) she is a wife, mom, friend, avid gardener, walker of a giant dog, and keeper of many (many!) pets. She also writes dark urban fantasy under the name of Lydia M. Hawke.

You can find Linda on her website at LindaPoitevin.com (sign up for her newsletter there to get book updates!) or shoot her an email (she loves to hear from readers!) at info@LindaPoitevin.com.

www.ingramcontent.com/pod-product-compliance
Lightning Source LLC
Chambersburg PA
CBHW030528080526
44586CB00011B/357